ALSO BY LOIS WYSE

NONFICTION
Nesting
Just Like Grandma Used to Make
Friend to Friend
Women Make the Best Friends
You Wouldn't Believe What My Grandchild Did
Grandmother's Pleasures
Grandmother's Treasures
Grandchildren Are So Much Fun I Should Have Had Them First
Funny, You Don't Look Like a Grandmother
Mrs. Success
Lovetalk
The Six-Figure Woman
Company Manners

FICTION
Seconds
The Granddaughter
Kiss, Inc.
Far from Innocence
The Rosemary Touch

POETRY
Love Poems for a Rainy Day
A Weeping Eye Can Never See
Are You Sure You Love Me?
Love Poems for the Very Married

Lois Wyse

Family Ties

the legacy of love

simon & schuster
new york london toronto sydney singapore

SIMON & SCHUSTER
Rockefeller Center
1230 Avenue of the Americas
New York, NY 10020

SIMON & SCHUSTER and colophon are registered trademarks
of Simon & Schuster, Inc.

Designed by Jeanette Olender
Manufactured in the United States of America

1   3   5   7   9   10   8   6   4   2

Library of Congress Cataloging-in-Publication Data
Wyse, Lois.
Family ties : the legacy of love / Lois Wyse.
p. cm.
1. Family—Anecdotes.   I. Title.
HQ734.W97 2001   306.85—dc21   2001017005
ISBN: 978-1-4767-3842-0

With thanks to John Mack Carter

for the opportunities he has given me
and for the privilege of being tied into his large,
loving family of Carters, editors, writers,
and friends

CONTENTS

Introduction   11

PART ONE   The Children's Hour

First Words   17
Family Stories   18
The Gifted Child   21
The Awful Tooth   26
The Diplomat   28
Sister Act   33
Sisters Again   37
Small-Town Boy   41
The Children Deserve a Good Life   44
Her Father's Daughter   48
Generations of Love   53
Family Dinner   59

PART TWO   Mom's the Word

Mother Load   63
The New, Improved Mother   64

Pioneer Mother   66

I Remember Your Mother   71

The Popcorn Report   73

What Do We Tell the Children?   79

Not a Word About This, Mother   84

Occupation: Mother   91

Are You Cheryl Doe?   95

Design for Living   105

PART THREE   The Legacy of Love

The Family   109

Bonjour, Lolo   110

Welcome to Paradise   117

Trouble in Paradise   120

Cousin Cuisine   122

Shopping Italian-Style   128

French Lights   134

The Gentleman Caller   138

Isn't France a Topless Country?   143

The Family at Play   145

Acknowledgments   153

INTRODUCTION

There are no applications, interviews, or previous experiences required for the job you'll hold all your life—the job of family member.

We are born to be sons and daughters and we are handed a collection of relatives. Then, as if it weren't tough enough playing with the family cards we're dealt at birth, we go ahead and create families of our own. Sometimes it's through marriage; sometimes it's through friendships that take on the characteristics of family ("Why didn't you call?" "Are you okay?" "Happy birthday.")

Sometimes the family is a blessing, sometimes a chore. Still, nothing in life lightens, brightens, or frightens us more than our family ties.

So here's to the family.

Here's to the mothers and daughters, the fathers and sons, the sisters and brothers, the aunts and uncles, the collections of cousins and grandparents and grandkids.

Here's to the halves, the steps, and the wholes.

Here's to the core of life, the family, and the histories and stories we make together.

Family Ties

Part One

The Children's Hour

FIRST WORDS

There is not a great deal one knows about a child until he or she stops screaming and begins saying real words.

It is possible to draw a small social history of a family, however, just by hearing the first word a child utters.

Bye
The first word of a child with two working parents
No
Look around—there's an older sibling in the house
Dada
A father who used his parental leave
Mama
Traditional family-style
Book
Upwardly mobile grandparents who visit often
Woof
City child who is pushed in pram by nanny and converses only with dogs

FAMILY STORIES

"Tennis is just a game; family is forever."
Serena Williams when asked how she felt competing against
her sister in the semifinals at Wimbledon.

His father was indeed the prototype of the Boston Brahmin, an aloof patriarch who maintained what his son termed "a close distance" from his children. During his growing-up years, the son never remembered any outward display of affection on his father's part.

Last year Father turned eighty-three, and from that day he has spoken to his son daily and concludes every conversation with "I love you."

Is that because of newly realized affection or the dropping of barriers that precluded the mention of love between men? Or is it simply that the father realizes, at last, that he truly loves his son?

The son really doesn't care about the reason; he's content with the love.

. . .

HE HAD five adult sons, and she had five adult sons, and they brought the ten together for Thanksgiving dinner the first year of their marriage. They also invited his ninety-nine-year-old mother, who sat at the head of the table.

What no one bothered to explain to Grandmother was that they had also invited the significant others of the ten, and since four of the ten sons were gay, there were only six women at the table.

As the turkey was carved, Grandmother looked down at the long line of men and asked, "Where are the girls?"

One of the sons was beginning to explain when Father lifted his hand. "Not now," he admonished. "You're sixty years too late."

ONE LOVELY spring day Gwyneth Paltrow, the actress, and I were asked to speak to young mothers about family and home. Gwyneth painted a picture of a family tied to complementary career paths, a family united by love. After we finished talking, we agreed to accept questions. The members of the audience, however, delighted as they were by Gwyneth's accessibility and openness, were reluctant to stand and question the celebrity.

So I moved forward and said I would ask the first question. "You've spoken of the closeness of your family. So I would like to ask what life lessons you learned from your parents."

Without hesitation she answered, "From my father I learned the importance of truth and integrity in all parts of life, and from my mother I learned to keep my room clean."

WHEN THEY were growing up, the three brothers never thought about going into business together, yet when each graduated from college, he found himself drifting into the family business, "just until I know what I want to do."

Now the three run the business, "and the business works just like the family," the middle brother explained. "The oldest tells the two of us what to do; it's just the way it was when we were kids. And we fight all the time. But let somebody from the outside come and say one word against one of the brothers to the others, and we'll band together and kill. I tell you, we never got off the playground, only now the playground is a lot bigger."

THE GIFTED CHILD

Hoover was known as the boy with a talent as big as Los Angeles. At eight months he began talking; at the age of two his vocabulary included everything from aardvark (which he could spell) to zebra (which he could draw). Then at the age of three his real gift became apparent. He could write; he didn't just make words, he communicated ideas. Generally, Hoover wrote poems, but there were also stories, essays, and for good measure, ideas for a play or two.

Rita wasn't sure how their son got so smart. "Harvey," she often said, "is it your family? It sure isn't mine. My dad spent his whole life on the Ford assembly line and my mother comes from a long line of housewives. Is there anybody in your family who ever painted a picture or wrote a book?"

At first Harvey tried looking back through the family he remembered. He was the first college graduate in his family. Since he'd gone to the state university, three other cousins had followed. But none of them were what anyone could label genius. "Nice, hardworking folks are all I remember," he told his wife. "I'm not sure how we got this kid. It's scary. I think he may be too smart for us."

"It's a challenge," Rita said. "We have to keep him stimulated. The girls in my office told me about some special schools, but I don't want a freaky kid. Let's just let him grow up with the kids in our neighborhood."

So Hoover went to public school with the kids on the street. By the time he reached the fourth grade he was writing at eighth-grade level, but his work in other subjects was not nearly so outstanding. "He only does what he likes," Rita said to Harvey. "How can we make him understand that life isn't just about doing the stuff you like?"

Hoover spent a lot of his time after school at the computer. "What are you doing?" his father would ask.

"Getting story ideas," he'd answer.

But Harvey prodded him. "Don't you ever have to study things like science?"

"It's too boring," Hoover answered.

"If you want to be a writer, you'll have to know a lot of things," his mother advised.

"I don't want to be a science writer," Hoover said, pushing his glasses back on to his nose.

Then one day Hoover's teacher called and asked his mother to come in for a special conference.

His mother sensed something was in the air, so she was slightly apprehensive when she went into the classroom after school.

"You know Hoover is a gifted child," the teacher began, "and this is why I am so concerned. He turned in a science paper with words and concepts even he couldn't know or understand. I went to the computer and found his paper——word for word——on the Internet. I told him I knew what he had done, but he doesn't think it's such a big deal. He said a lot of people get their ideas from the Internet. I tried to explain that it's one thing to get an idea from someone's work; it's quite another to use it word for word. But I don't think that Hoover understood what I said. He seemed to think I was a dummy."

Rita shook her head; she could barely speak. She was almost afraid to talk to Hoover. She wasn't sure what she'd say and how much she'd regret anything she said now.

With a heavy heart, Rita called Harvey. "What should I do?" she asked.

"I have to think about it, honey," he answered. "But don't do anything right now. Don't say anything to him. I'll come up with an answer by tonight. I promise you."

For the first time since she left the school, Rita felt a sense of relief. Harvey was a man of his word. She could trust him to do the right thing.

After dinner that night Harvey turned to his son. "I want to go up to the library and get some new books. Why don't you walk with me, Hoover, and we'll stop for some ice cream?"

Hoover smiled. He thought that was a pretty good idea.

As they neared the library, Hoover's father asked, "How are things at school?"

"Okay. I wrote a new story, Dad."

"Did you also write a science paper, Hoover?"

Hoover turned crimson. Dad knew.

"Do you have any idea why I'm asking this, son?"

"Because Mom went to school today?"

"Partly. Let's sit here on this bench for a minute."

"Dad, I didn't do anything wrong. The Internet is there for everybody."

"To use, not to abuse."

"What do you mean?"

"Let's put it this way. You expect to be a writer. Well, suppose your story was published and someone came along and just took your words and used them and never said they were yours. Would you like that?"

"No."

"There is something called artistic integrity, Hoover. No matter how great or small your talent is, you must always be faithful to yourself as an artist. That means your work must always be your work, not a copy of someone else's. And when you do get ideas from another source, you must give credit to the original thinker. All of us would have liked it better if you'd said you didn't understand the science project and couldn't do the work rather than copy a sophisticated essay that had concepts everyone knew you couldn't possibly have grasped."

Hoover looked soberly at his father. "I think I get it."

"Okay, Hoover," his father answered, "then let's do what we came out to do. Books and ice cream. There's nothing better in life."

Hoover slipped his hand into his father's. "You're really smart, Dad."

THE AWFUL TOOTH

We called her Baby Emily because we knew she'd be the last baby in the family, and we wanted to keep her baby-hood a fact for as long as we could. But on her fourth birthday Baby Emily made an announcement. She was no longer to be called Baby Emily. She said with confidence and amazing self-assurance that she was now to be known as Emily.

But we weren't ready to call her Emily until the unexpected occurred. A few weeks after her birthday Emily lost her first baby tooth. Even her great-grandmother hadn't heard of a child losing a tooth at the age of four.

But if news of the tooth came as a surprise, what followed came as a shock. Emily looked at the tooth that, until minutes ago, had been wiggling in her mouth. First she cried, and then she screamed hysterically.

Denise, her mother, comforted her with motherly words. "It's all right. You know you're a big girl now, so it's okay to be the first one of your friends to lose a tooth."

But Emily only became more agitated.

Her mother cuddled her. "Emily, this isn't making any sense. Now, tell me why you're so upset."

Emily finally choked the words between sobs. "Mommy, I don't want to put my tooth under my pillow and have some stranger come into my room. I only want my family in my room."

So Denise carefully, gently undid the generations of mythmaking and told her daughter the truth about the Tooth Fairy.

"Parents can't win," Denise observed. "We are so careful to teach our children to avoid strangers; then our sons and daughters pour their milk from cartons with pictures of missing children—and dutifully we reinforce the lessons and remind them that no, they must never talk to strangers. So as I think about this, I'm not surprised that Emily was upset about a stranger coming into her home. I'm surprised only that more children aren't worried."

As for Emily's father, he handed her the dollar, was rewarded with her gap-toothed smile, and thought he ought to remind more fathers that a loving daddy can still bring more joy than Santa, the Easter Bunny, or even the Tooth Fairy.

THE DIPLOMAT

Five-year-old Elizabeth sat in a chair and looked silently at the two adults who were now lost in their own thoughts. For days now Elizabeth had been the silent witness to the prolonged pauses of the men and women Father had known as they came to visit Mummy on her return to New York.

It was while the family was in Majorca on holiday from Father's duties at the embassy that he had become ill. Somehow everything had taken place at night, long after Elizabeth's bedtime, but she had pieced the events together. Father became so ill that no one could help him, and then Mummy told her that Father had gone to heaven and was going to watch over her. But Elizabeth wasn't quite sure how Father would know where to look for her, since they were moving back to the United States.

Now they were living in the apartment Mummy had lived in before she'd married Father, and every day people stopped by to "pay their respects and welcome dear Katrina back to New York."

Most of the people came and smiled sympathetically at

Elizabeth, who sat in her small straight-backed chair. Like the diplomat's daughter she was trained to be, Elizabeth stood at each introduction, smiled stiffly, and curtsied. Invariably the adults smiled in return and went back to their own grown-up conversations.

Today's visitor was yet another diplomat. Elizabeth went through her usual polite performance and then sat primly watching, but not hearing, as he and her mother chatted. She was surprised when Mummy's soft voice repeated, "Elizabeth, I think you should answer Ambassador Williams. He has just offered a lovely invitation."

"I beg your pardon," Elizabeth said quickly. "I'm afraid I didn't hear you."

"Elizabeth, I am an old friend of your father, and I have known your mother for many years. It would give me great pleasure if I could be your friend, too. I have lived in New York for a long time, and I would like very much to be a guide for you here. I'd like to show you all the lovely things we have for children. There is a zoo in Central Park, for instance."

Elizabeth, who had already seen the animals at F.A.O. Schwarz, had a question. "Please, are the animals real?"

"Indeed. And there are many other adventures. I will

take you on a boat ride and show you places in the city that will make you think you are in another country."

Elizabeth looked questioningly at her mother.

Katrina nodded. "It's a lovely offer, Elizabeth."

"Then thank you. I should like this very much."

IN THE WEEKS that followed, the ambassador introduced Elizabeth to the childhood pleasures of New York and, along the way, learned about the childhood of the little girl he was shepherding. She liked to be in the kitchen with the cook, remembered the gardens at the embassy, and missed having her own little garden to tend.

Elizabeth, in turn, learned a bit about the ambassador. He had been married but his wife had died in an airplane crash a year after their wedding. He'd never married again, so he had no children, but he was uncle to his sister's daughter and son and had taken them touring in New York a few years earlier, just as he was now doing with Elizabeth.

"Then you're not married?"

The ambassador shook his head. Elizabeth thought he seemed sad. "Then you must come to us for dinner on Saturday," she said.

. . .

SATURDAY EVENING Mummy answered the door. The ambassador stood there with a small bunch of French violets. "How charming," Mummy said. "Stay a few minutes, won't you? Elizabeth will be here soon, and you can give her the flowers yourself."

"These aren't for Elizabeth," he answered. "They're for you. I realize Elizabeth was the one who invited me tonight for dinner . . ."

"I beg your pardon," Katrina said. "I think you just said you were invited for dinner this evening."

"Yes. My heavens, Katrina. It was Elizabeth's invitation, but I thought she'd told you."

Mummy laughed affectionately. "No, she didn't, John, but do stay."

When Elizabeth came home, she found Mummy and the ambassador sipping cocktails. Elizabeth smiled.

BY THE TIME she was in the third grade, Elizabeth realized that her life was compartmentalized in just the ways she wanted. There was Mummy; there were her school friends; and interacting with both was the ambassador, who often took her to dinner with Mummy and always let her bring a friend along when he showed her yet another wonder of New York.

The next year, when the ambassador and Katrina decided to marry, her headmistress said to Elizabeth, "How nice that you will have a stepfather."

"I am not going to have a stepfather," Elizabeth said, correcting her teacher carefully. "I am going to have a family."

SISTER ACT

This is a story about sisters who didn't have to work together in order to work together.

The Simon sisters grew up in a household where success was brewed in the morning coffee. Their father, Richard Simon, was the co-founder of Simon & Schuster, and their childhood memories are filled with the famous names of those they met at home at their parents' parties.

The girls grew up and, amazingly, all went on to become famous names themselves. There's Carly the singer, Lucy the composer, and Joanna the opera singer.

This particular story began when Joanna retired from the opera and moved to a new career covering the arts scene for the *McNeil-Lehrer NewsHour* on PBS. There she decided to interview Marcia Norman, who had won a Pulitzer Prize for her play *'Night, Mother.*

During the course of the interview Joanna asked, "What are you writing now?"

"A musical," Ms. Norman replied. Then, in an aside, she asked, "Since you're an opera singer, do you know someone who could write the score, someone who can write for opera?"

"Why opera?"

"Because this is a musical adaptation of *The Secret Garden,* and I hear an operatic score."

Joanna took a deep breath. "Now, don't think I'm being pushy, but I do happen to know the one perfect person for this job——my sister Lucy."

Ms. Norman didn't say yes, but she didn't say no.

When the interview ended, Joanna rushed to call Lucy. "I just found the best job in the world for you. Sit tight. You are about to get a call from Marcia Norman."

Days went by. No call.

Lucy called Joanna. "I've been sitting tight. Nothing happened."

"Wait," Joanna advised.

And then three days later, just the way it does in the movies, the call from Marcia Norman came.

Lucy wrote a sample song and the producers said, "Very nice, but we think we want a famous composer from London."

When the famous composer shook his famous head in

the negative, Lucy was asked to write another audition song.

The producers loved it. Would she do another song?

Lucy called her sister. "I am writing this show one audition song at a time."

After the third test song, Lucy picked up her head, put down her foot, and told the producers that the time had come for them to reach a decision. Now it was all or nothing.

They said, "All."

Finally Lucy had the job her sister knew all along she should have.

And what a job Lucy did.

The Secret Garden won the Tony, has gone on to major productions in Australia and by the Royal Shakespeare Company, and is seen each year by countless thousands in regional theaters.

During the writing of *The Secret Garden* Marcia and Lucy became not only partners but close friends as well. Along the way they learned that they had a secret that they shared: a wish to make a musical of one of their favorite books, *Wuthering Heights*. So now, in addition to keeping their first musical fresh and checking the production values, they also spend time lost in the melodic moors of Wuthering Heights.

The Simon sisters are often asked if their parents had a formula for raising successful children.

Joanna says, "I don't remember our parents ever wanting us to be exceptional. What I do remember is that anytime any of us came home with a lump of clay that was supposed to be a sculpture or a scrap of paper with a story or a song, they made a huge fuss over us. But when it came to report cards, our parents just shrugged. They weren't very interested in grades."

SISTERS AGAIN

Marilyn and I grew up tied in each other's hair ribbons. Our mothers were best friends, so what could be better for the two mothers than to encourage their daughters to be best friends, too?

But we became more than friends; we were pretend sisters, the sisters neither of us had. In the fashion of the time, she called my parents Uncle Roy and Aunt Rose, and her mother and father were my Aunt Edie and Uncle Seymour.

Our families went on picnics and visited back and forth, and we even called all our grandmothers Grandma and our grandfathers Grandpa. I couldn't imagine any life or secret that Marilyn didn't share.

But then I turned eleven or so, and Marilyn moved to another school district, and lo and behold! The friendship didn't travel well. We found other girls who'd play our games and share our giggles. And after a while Marilyn and her family moved to California. Sometimes Aunt Edie came back to Cleveland to visit, but Marilyn was going to college by then and had her own life to manage. So we didn't see one another; our mothers kept in better touch than we did.

I do remember visiting Marilyn and her husband, Paul, when my children were toddlers; we went to California and took our children to play with hers. They played nicely but didn't seem to have that same spark for one another that Marilyn and I had had. After that trip, although we both enjoyed visiting with each other, Marilyn and I just didn't stay in close communication. Who has time to write letters when kids are crying, meals are waiting to be made, and somebody needs a Band-Aid or a glass of water?

So I didn't think often of Marilyn, and after a while I couldn't even remember her married name.

And then one day my son Rob met a cousin of Marilyn's who remembered me from his childhood, remembered me as Marilyn's best friend who was always playing at her house.

Just hearing Marilyn's name made me aware of a void in my life. Why hadn't I ever noticed that there was a hole where Marilyn's love had been? It wasn't that I didn't have dear friends. I did and still do. It was just that—well, growing up with someone just is not the same as being a grown-up with someone.

Rob gave me Marilyn's name and telephone number, and then I had cold feet. What if Marilyn had purposely avoided calling all these years because she didn't want to talk to me? What if her life had hit a big bump that she didn't want to share? Both Uncle Seymour and Aunt Edie were gone, and I had heard from my mother that Aunt Edie's death had crushed Marilyn's spirit for a time. For months I held on to the number without making a call. And then on February 12, Marilyn's birthday, I made a decision. I would call that day or stop thinking about her.

In the morning I dialed her number. "Marilyn, this is a voice from your past."

"Lois," she said in that familiar Ohio twang (like mine). "You won't believe it, but today is my birthday."

"Mair," I answered, "you won't believe it, but I know."

And then we both cried.

We cried for what had been, what is, and what we know we mean to each other.

THAT WAS a few years and a thousand e-mails ago. Now we are in constant communication. We know about each of our joys and our sorrows, and we share them in a sisterly spirit that continues to flourish from its beginnings.

We've visited each other in our homes. Just the two of us once went to a spa for a week together. We jog our memories with "remember"—but mostly we talk about the "is" of life rather than the "was."

Once in a while we need to ask each other about something that happened in a time and place only we can remember. As Marilyn said, "Isn't it wonderful to be sisters again?" And I nodded mutely. Sometimes things are so good in a family that you just can't talk about them.

SMALL-TOWN BOY

John Mack Carter and his twin sister, Carolyn, grew up in the small town of Murray, Kentucky, where their daddy was the superintendent of schools and their mama was a schoolteacher. From the get-go, both the Carter children knew that education was going to be a significant part of their lives. What John didn't realize at the time was that his career path would take him from Kentucky, and his children would take him even farther.

After he graduated from college, John went to work in the Midwest for a major publisher, eventually moved to New York, and, in succession, became the editor of three major women's magazines: *McCall's, Ladies' Home Journal,* and *Good Housekeeping.*

As an editor John was known both for his innovative ideas and for his genuine interest in and kindness toward his staff. And as a father to the children he and his wife, Sharlyn, had——well, sometimes John Mack was an attentive father and sometimes, like other dads of the 1950s, he was away on business or working late. In other words, there were days and nights when Dad wasn't there. Still, the children grew up feeling close to their father and knew they could confide in him.

While still a student at Fordham, son John came home one day and told his parents he was going to marry a fellow student, a girl named Victoria. "By the way," he added, "she's Spanish."

Although Victoria and her parents lived in the United States, the family maintained a residence in La Coruña, in Spain, and each year brought the family's nine children back to Spain, where they all visited. Victoria expected her husband and the children born to them to accompany her. They did, and over the years John found that he had some of his best times with Victoria and their children on these visits. Then one day John had an idea. If these visits had cemented John's feelings for Victoria's family, why not use one trip to truly integrate his two families, the one into which he was born and the family of his wife and children?

So John suggested to his parents that they accompany Victoria, him, and their children to Spain for a real family visit.

John Mack and Sharlyn were intrigued. But they weren't sure how they'd feel once they arrived.

"I guess I didn't expect to feel a sense of belonging," John Mack said later. "Victoria's family is part of an ancient community. I think we're old-timers because our Kentucky relatives go back a few generations. Here are people who can trace their roots to the seventeenth century, who took us to places where their names are carved in stone on buildings. Still, we all looked at one another, at our grandchildren, and we knew we were family. At lunch one day a cousin of Victoria's reached into his pocket and asked, 'Want to see my family tree?' Out came eighty-five names——and that was just first cousins.

"It was an astonishing trip. Here is my son, part of a world family, and he has brought us along and introduced us so that our own family now has boundaries beyond our expectations. John did an amazing thing for us: by arranging this trip he made us understand how complex yet how unified our family is."

THE MIXING and melding will never stop in the Carter family. Says John, "Sharlyn and I can't wait to go with our daughter Jonna to meet the family of her husband. John Low was born in Shanghai; he's Chinese." Then he laughed. "Some new world for a small-town boy, isn't it?"

THE CHILDREN DESERVE
A GOOD LIFE

It was one of the best stores in town, and Columbine knew she was lucky to have a job there as a fitter. The ladies were particular, it was true, but the clothes were expensive, and as any good seamstress knows, it's easier to fix clothes when the seams are generous and the fabric supple.

Columbine was young and energetic and had a pretty smile and a soft manner. Soon she came to know some of the shop's best clients, who regularly asked for her when alterations were necessary.

"It's Mrs. Grant in Fitting Room One," a saleswoman announced to Columbine. "She wants you. She's a nice woman, but only you seem to have the patience to make her feel that she looks like a size eight when she wears a size twelve."

Columbine smiled and took her pins and tape.

"Oh, Mrs. Grant, that's a beautiful suit," Columbine said. Indeed it was. The black silk shimmered, and it truly made Mrs. Grant more sylphlike.

Now it was Columbine's job to make the suit work better for the customer. With her practiced eye, she knew immediately that she would raise the shoulders, lower the hem, and fix the cuffs. Columbine sighed and sat on the floor to start the hem. It would take a good ten minutes for the fitting, and she knew Mrs. Grant was certain to reconsider even after the pinning was complete.

"I'm going to wear the suit for the holidays when my daughter comes home. She went away to school this year and I am so lonesome."

Columbine didn't answer. She had a mouthful of pins.

"Nobody understands how hard it is for a mother to see her daughter go away. My husband doesn't understand, and my friends think I should be happy, but I'm not. You have young children so you can't know what I'm talking about." Mrs. Grant seemed near tears.

Columbine got to her feet. "I am so sorry for you, Mrs. Grant. You see, I do know what it feels like."

"How would you know with such young children? Isn't your oldest about twelve? Just last year you had another one, didn't you?"

Columbine sighed. "I never talked about it, but I lived for seven years without my two older boys. When my first son was five, I became pregnant again. Then after the baby was born, my husband and I couldn't find a place to live. We were in one room, and we knew that if we wanted our boys to have a good life, we would both have to go to work. But we couldn't afford anyone to help with our children. Both our parents live in Colombia. What could we do? I talked to my mother, and she said that she and my father would take our two boys until we were able to care for them.

"I will never forget flying the children there and leaving them. I cried all the way home. My husband and I both got jobs, and we started to spend every cent we could to call the children and talk to them. My mother is a very good woman, and she promised me she would keep showing pictures of us to the boys and remind them of who we were, but month after month we never had enough money to go back to see them. The older boy remembered us, of course, and when I talked to my baby, the one I hadn't seen since he was a year old, I kept telling him I was mama. Finally, after three years we saved enough to visit them. When I saw my little one, he ran from me. 'But I'm your mama,' I told him. 'No,' he said, pointing to my mother, 'that's my mama.' He was too little to understand.

"After a month I went back to the United States and still had to leave my boys with my mother. Then two years ago I became pregnant and had my third child. My mother said, 'I will take him, too.' 'No,' I told her. 'We will figure out a way to keep our boys.'

"My husband and I talked, and we decided that he would work nights and I would get a day job. We would bring our two boys back and raise the three. We would be a family. Believe me, the happiest day of my life was the day we took our baby and went back to Colombia and brought all three boys home to live with us. So, yes, Mrs. Grant, I know what it is to be lonely for a child."

"Columbine, I had no idea what you sacrificed to give your boys a better life."

Columbine shook her head. "I had no idea what a better life really was. It isn't about a nice house. We still live in a little place, but you know what? Now we have a nice family. Finally we are giving them a good life."

HER FATHER'S DAUGHTER

For days Judith had been unable to concentrate on anything except the phone call from her father in Israel informing her that his longtime partner and best friend had not only dissolved their business relationship but had accused her father of stealing. She could barely think the word, much less comprehend its meaning. How could her father, the kindest and gentlest of men, be capable of committing a crime? Cheating his partner? Taking a sum of money the partner had earmarked for his son in Paris and, instead of delivering it to the son, keeping it for himself? Never. Not Papa.

"Fight him," Judith had shouted on the phone when she heard what was happening.

"How?" Papa had asked mournfully. "The only way to answer him is with a document that proves I gave the check to his son. The document is in a Paris bank."

"Help Papa," Judith begged her two sisters by phone.

"How?" they asked. "We don't know anything about French banks or French law. You're the one who's living in Paris now. You ought to be able to do something."

For the first time in her life Judith realized that everyone in her family had lost control of the situation. It was up to her to do something. Anything. She called her father. "Tell me the whole story, please."

"It's not much of a story. I think my partner wanted the business for himself and his family, so he said that when I took money to Paris for him to give to his son——"

"How much money?" Judith interrupted.

"Three hundred and fifty dollars——"

"You mean this man is vilifying you for three hundred and fifty dollars?" Her father assented glumly. "He says that instead of giving the money to his son I kept it for myself. But I went to the bank with his son, they gave us a receipt, and I turned the money over to his son."

"Where is the receipt?" Judith asked.

"I don't know. I guess I gave it back to my partner to show that his son did get the cash. But I don't have the receipt."

"If you had a bank receipt, then the bank must have a record of it," Judith insisted.

"I called, but they say they keep records only for a short period of time. Now there is a trial coming up and my life will end with a scandal that I didn't cause. You will all be disgraced forever because of me." A sob escaped her father's throat.

Judith listened in fear; she had never known Papa to cry. "Think for a minute, Papa. Where is the bank in Paris? Which one? I am going to go there and get the receipt."

"How can you do that?" her father asked.

"Because I must," she answered tersely.

JUDITH MADE a schedule. The trial was to begin in five days. She would have three days to get the receipt, another day to have copies made, and a day to fly back to Israel. If she was lucky, she'd be back before the trial began.

The first morning Judith went to the bank when it opened. She went to a counter and said she needed a receipt for a transaction five years earlier.

"We don't keep records here," the bank officer said.

Judith felt her brain hum. *Here.* That was the operative word. "If not here, then where?" Judith asked.

"In vaults outside Paris," the officer said.

"I need to go there," Judith said.

"You cannot," she was told in French.

"I must," she repeated.

"You cannot," she was told once more.

"Then let me see your manager," she responded.

"He is busy. Why don't you just sit over there on that bench and his assistant will take you to see him when he's free." So Judith sat and waited. And waited. Three hours later she was still waiting. She could feel the tears roll down her cheeks when the door opened and a man strode from the office. When he saw her, he stopped. "I am the manager," he said gently. "What is your problem?"

Judith caught her breath and quickly told her story.

"If we can help, we must," the manager said. "I know where we keep those records. I will send for them. Come back here tomorrow."

The next day Judith went back.

No, they had not yet found the records. Come back to-morrow, she was told.

But I have no time, she explained.

We have no papers, they replied.

Four days later the papers were found; the receipt with Papa's name and the son's signature was there. But the trial was already beginning.

Judith put the precious paper in her handbag, went to the airport, and took the next plane home. "This is like the movies," she told the cab driver when she landed. "Get me to the courthouse immediately."

She ran up the steps into the courtroom and handed the paper to her father's attorney. Within minutes the suit was dismissed.

I WILL TAKE Judith back to the airport myself," Papa said the next day. Sitting next to her father, Judith felt her father's authority return. Once again he was a man in command of himself, his family, their lives. How different from a week ago, she thought.

Silently the two drove. As they reached the airport Papa reached over and put his arm around Judith. "I always wanted a son," he said. Pausing, he hugged her in gratitude and then added with the booming laugh she remembered, "but a daughter like you will do."

GENERATIONS OF LOVE

Put yourself in Dana's shoes. You have a good, solid family: a caring husband, four kids, three of them in college, and then one day you get a phone call from Julie, your fourth child, an eighteen-year-old you love and adore. But this daughter, not one to follow the steps of her older siblings, is living on a commune in Arizona. She has gone her own way, and it becomes perfectly clear she's made a decision for herself as she announces, "I'm having a baby. The father comes from a very fine family, so it will be a good baby. But I don't want to get married. I just want to love my baby, and the women in my commune want me to have a baby because they can't."

Dana felt the kind of panic any mother would feel at that kind of news. Still, she realized that the call was Julie's version of a cry for help. Dana booked the next flight to Arizona. Her daughter needed and wanted her, and she had to follow her heart, fly to her child, and try to reason with her. The decision wasn't just about Julie now. How could her baby raise a baby?

Dana spent a week with her daughter, and by the time she was ready to leave, Julie had agreed that no, she really couldn't raise a child. The child must be adopted, so together the mother and daughter arranged to have the unborn child taken by one of the women who had befriended her.

THE YEARS went by; Julie was now a musician and cabaret singer. Yet there was never a day when Julie didn't wonder about the baby her heart had named Rebecca. Julie thought about Rebecca even as her work took her to other cities and to Europe. She thought of her even as she played with different musical groups. Then she met Gus, also a musician. They married, had a daughter, Samantha, and after a few years, divorced. Now Julie and Samantha became a team of their own, and the visits to Dana became more frequent. Yet Julie could not forget Rebecca. From time to time she called Rebecca's adoptive mother and visited with the child.

And then one day Rebecca's adoptive mother called Julie. "She's sixteen and I can't handle her. She wants to live with you."

Instinctively Julie said, "Send her to me," and then she thought about what she'd said so quickly. What would Rebecca's presence mean? Samantha knew about Rebecca, but how would she feel about her coming into their lives now? How would her parents handle a grandchild they'd forgotten existed? Could her siblings love a niece they'd never known? What was she doing to all of them?

Frightened and uncertain, Julie talked it over with Samantha, now twelve. "What do you think?" Julie asked.

"We have a great family for her," Samantha assured her mother. "Besides, I always wanted a big sister."

"Well, we're supposed to go to visit Grandma and Grandpa with all the cousins for Christmas," Julie remembered. "Do you think we ought to go? The cousins don't know about Rebecca."

"Call Grandma," Samantha answered quickly. "She always knows what to do."

THIS TIME, however, Grandma Dana didn't know what to do; at least she didn't know when Julie called, because Grandma hadn't even known that Julie was in contact with Rebecca. "I'll call you back tomorrow," she said quickly.

Then Grandma and Grandpa had a conversation. "We can't bring that child into the family immediately with all the cousins," Grandma said. "It would be cruel to have a young girl come face-to-face with this houseful of people who are her relatives. And it will be too confusing for the cousins and the aunts and uncles."

"And me," Grandpa added.

The next day Grandma called Julie. "I have a plan, Julie. Much as I'd love to have all of you here, I think it's best if you not come for Christmas. Instead, I'll visit you the week before Christmas and meet Rebecca. Then, in a few weeks, we'll all make arrangements for you and your girls to visit your brother. After that you'll all see each of your sisters and their children in their homes. By spring vacation the whole family will be able to get together at our house, and everyone will understand and know your expanded family."

Grandma called her other children and brought them up to speed. "It's been a long time since we've had a teenager in the family," she reminded them, "and while Grandpa and I are certainly ready to give love, I'm not sure we'll have the kind of advice Julie may want over the next few years. We'll all need to help one another. Will you all get involved?"

"Help our sister? Of course," one sister answered. The other siblings agreed, and within weeks they opened their hearts and homes. Rebecca came to visit them in each of their homes and sought their advice in making decisions about everything from her education to her wardrobe.

IT IS NOT always easy for us, so we take it a day at a time," Dana says thoughtfully. "This child is still looking for her place in a family that didn't know her for sixteen years, and everyone is trying to find a comfortable space for her."

Will there be a happy ending?

"I think there's a good chance there will be," says Dana, "because of the aunts and uncles and cousins who are giving Rebecca the kind of everyday love she wants, and they are listeners and advisers for Julie.

"I think one reason that Rebecca came back to Julie is that she wanted more than a mother figure. She was aware that Julie and Samantha were part of this big, loving family, and she wanted to be included. If there are any heroes here, they are Julie's siblings. I am so proud of them for opening their arms, for being caring and concerned.

"Isn't the knowledge that the children we raise are capable of giving this kind of love the real reward of family?"

FAMILY DINNER

I look around the table
And see those who mean
The most to me.

So why are my eyes
Filled with tears?

Because I also see
Those who are not there.

Part Two

Mom's
the Word

MOTHER LOAD

In the beginning
The hardest part of
Mothering
Is making more of the job,
Smothering
With do's and don'ts and shouldn'ts.

Then one day
We awake to find the role reduced to
Othering,
As other voices, other friends, other teachers
Lay claim to babies who once heard only us.

Still the job does not end
Just because the childhood does.
Like the washer and dryer
We start at heavy-duty,
Recycle when needed,
But always keep the motor
In good running order.

THE NEW, IMPROVED
MOTHER

"Hi, Debbie. How are you?"

"Great, Dad. Let me talk to Mom, please."

Chuck flipped the phone to his wife and listened as Sharon, with her newly adopted voice of authority, said, "Oh, that's funny, Debbie. No, relax. That's nothing to worry about. The baby is just like you were at that age. Isn't that amazing? Maybe there really is something to heredity. Oh yes, I can hear him. Go ahead, dear. Call back later."

"Can't she do anything without you?" Chuck asked when Sharon turned back to him.

Sharon smiled a small, self-satisfied smile. "Chuck," she said, "do you realize how long it's taken our daughter to think I'm something besides a roadblock to her happiness? For years I was the one who screamed each day, 'Stand up straight, lose weight, study more, come in early, get interested in sports, buy new underwear, don't cry, girls don't always mean what they say, save yourself for the right man and don't get in trouble with the wrong one.' And let's not forget that I was the one who told her she'd better not get a tattoo or put a ring in her nose if she wanted to come into this house again.

"Now that she's safely married and a new mother, my role has gone from police mom to adviser mom. I am not just Debbie's mother. I am her baby's grandmother. All Debbie wants now is to seek my advice. 'What should he eat? What should he wear? Why is he crying?' "

Chuck smiled. "So how do you plan to handle this new advisory role?"

"Gently, dear. Very gently. I will give advice only when Debbie asks. As for the baby, I will never tell him what to do. He can slouch, eat disgusting snacks, stay out late, study whenever he feels like it. He can have anything he wants whenever he wants. After all, I don't have the time to wait for him to grow up so he can stand talking to me."

PIONEER MOTHER

She never crossed the country in a covered wagon, baked bread in a coal stove, or fought off the Indians, yet my mother is the true pioneer in our family.

Her life spanned most of the twentieth century, so that made her a witness to life during two world wars, the Great Depression, Lindbergh's solo flight, a man landing on the moon, the Scopes trial, Sacco-Vanzetti, Woodrow Wilson, Churchill, Hitler, Mussolini, and Tito, not to mention Rudolph Valentino, Elvis Presley, and Frank Sinatra. She survived them all. She also survived two husbands and the deaths of her parents, her sisters, and most of her best friends, as well as the premature passing of a stepson and son-in-law. Her counsel to me when I was distraught over the last illness of a close friend: "If you can survive the past, you can face the present."

Of course she was right. Even though daughters don't always agree with their mothers, Mother was probably right more times than I credit her with. Still, I often questioned her approach. Once, when she decided she wanted another house and my father was reluctant to move, she convinced him that her knees were aching too much to permit her to climb stairs. So they moved into a one-story house in the next suburb. A year later I asked if her knees were better. She laughed and said, "There was never anything wrong with my knees."

"But you said to Daddy——"

She dismissed me with a wave of her hand. "I said that because it was the only way I could get him to move. It's called a campaign, dear, and it was for his own good."

In fact, most of Mother's decisions were justified with the words, "It's for your own good."

She hovered over me, watched my every move, wanted to check every thought, and most of all, wanted to keep me close to home. She would not let me go to camp and didn't insist that I go to college. When, at age eighteen, I went to Columbia University Summer School for six weeks, she and my father showed up at the end of four weeks because they said they were too lonely without me.

But she led our family in some ways that changed my life for the better. She had a lifelong love of reading, and when I didn't even know my letters, she took me to the library and kept me going there until books became the center of my life. When I was in high school, she insisted I take typing courses, because "you'll have a way to earn a living." Although she was born at a time when women weren't expected to earn a living, she was prescient in that regard. She loved the theater, did crossword puzzles almost religiously, and started me on them to sharpen my vocabulary. (I still remember that an ai is a sloth, and syzygy is an alignment of celestial objects). We knitted together and made socks and sweaters for anyone who would let us. Late at night we played canasta; she was a smart card player, and I could see how her careful risk taking at the card table carried over into her life. She weighed possibilities carefully and taught me never to plunge into the unknown. Even after my father's death and after meeting a fine gentleman, a caring widower, she was reluctant to marry until she and I discussed the pros and cons.

But when she did remarry, Mother treated her new husband's son, David, and daughter-in-law, Eleanor, as warmly as she did my family. Following David's death she kept her relationship with Eleanor strong, and was my first role model as a stepmother.

But it is through her acceptance of life in her later years

that my mother has truly been the pioneer. When my father died, my mother—already a grandmother—had never written a check or driven a car. But she learned. She said that independence can begin when you let it. And so we have watched Mother move into her own old age, blazing the trail for all our family.

Who truly knows how to treat old age? As individuals, how would we know how to behave if we didn't have our mothers acting out the do's and don'ts for all of us?

We have had rocky times, my mother and I. When I took her car from her at age ninety, she told me firmly that I had robbed her of her independence and she was going to die. She added, "And it's all your fault." Of course, she continued to live—but she had to change a lot about her life, including moving to a home with assisted living. She was angry at first; five years later she admitted it was the best place for her.

Now, as I write this, she is unable to read, her hearing is less than good (despite her hearing aid), and she uses a walker to go to the dining room at the residence, but she plans her wardrobe and puts her clothes together for each appearance, applying her makeup with care. "I still think a woman has to look her best when she goes out," she says proudly. She misses the friends who are gone, but she does not mourn them every day.

So in her own way and with her own style, Mother is pioneering old age. Just as she led me to the library, she now guides me to this next stage with her own acquired wisdom. I watch, and from her I am learning that regardless of age, we'll all have to live life a day at a time, do the best we can, and complain as little as possible.

Thank you, Mother.

I REMEMBER YOUR
MOTHER

When Bobbie's mother died, the family decided to hold the funeral back in Richmond. After all, Mother had been one of the FFV, and the role of descendant of one of the First Families of Virginia was not one to be taken lightly.

It was a difficult time for Bobbie; she had wonderful, loving memories of her mother. But in going back to Richmond she found her grief sweetened by the recollections of others who'd loved and respected her mother. The funeral was practically a civic event. The governor was there, along with every community leader. And there were also lots of ladies with fichus at the neck, lorgnettes at the eye, and fond memories at the ready.

After the service, many people came to speak with Bobbie. The governor kissed her on the cheek; the mayor shook her hand. And the ladies—were there ever ladies like Southern ladies? With lavender-scented hankies, the ladies pressed Bobbie's hand and recalled her darling mother. "Your mother," began one of the ladies somewhat tearfully, "was one of the most beautiful women in Richmond. I can remember her coming-out party. She was the most beautiful debutante of the season. Of course, as my dear departed mother often said, 'Why not? She was the daughter of the belle of Richmond.' Yes, indeed. You come from a long line of beauties."

Then, withdrawing her hand slightly, the dowager smiled brightly at Bobbie. "And you, my dear," the lady continued, "look exactly like your father."

THE POPCORN REPORT

Faith Popcorn is a woman who spends most of her time in a place none of us has ever been: the future.

At least, that's how she has spent most of the past twenty years. But today the present, not the future, has an even stronger hold on the private life of America's most famous futurist. Faith has counseled companies from Procter & Gamble to Hasbro and she consistently advises marketers like McDonald's and IBM. She is the founder and head of BrainReserve, a New York–based consultancy, and the author of three respected best-sellers about market trends. Her business is run from a town house on New York's Upper East Side, and she has a small cottage in East Hampton, New York. But until recently Faith never spent much time at either of her residences; instead she found herself in airports, at client meetings, and juggling travel plans as she made a business grow.

Then one day a few years ago Faith felt—well, what did she feel? "I felt I wanted something different. It wasn't that I sensed there was something missing. I just knew that I wanted something else in my life. Earlier my best friend, Lys Marigold, adopted a Chinese baby girl. I really came to love her daughter, who is such a smart, beautiful child. I'm sure some of my feelings came because I was raised in Shanghai the first five years of my life. My father was an attorney with the United States Army, and until the family returned to the United States, I felt Chinese.

"I suppose some of my affection for those early years was surfacing when I decided to fill out the papers to adopt a Chinese girl, too. It's interesting, but Lys, not wanting to pressure me, didn't overly encourage me to go through with the adoption. She had been creative director of my company for twelve years, besides coauthoring my three books, so she knew firsthand how hard I worked. She didn't see how I could fit a baby into my travel schedule and work routine. She knew I'd have to make big adjustments to my life. We both realized that it was different for her; she's a writer who can work at home and control her hours.

"Even as I filled out the papers, I wasn't certain I'd follow through. Every day I thought, Gee, I'll call and cancel. I knew that if I did follow through, I'd need to make some life changes, so I promised myself I'd adopt only if I had a sign of some sort."

After a few months Faith was sent a picture of a little girl. She took one look at the picture and knew she had a first sign in the face of the child. "I looked at her, and I knew she needed me, and I needed her. Then I learned about a second sign; she had the same birthday at Lys's daughter, Skye Qi."

And so Faith, emboldened by the signs that she wanted, went to China for her child. "I thought about the changes I'd have to make," she recalled. "I wouldn't be able to work my ninety-hour weeks fifty-two weeks a year. I'd have to take more time at home. Oh yes, and speaking of home, that second-story office I was adding in East Hampton would become the nursery instead.

"As I went to China, I thought to myself that I know the future. I know how to turn a company around. I really know a lot of things, but when I got to China, I realized that I didn't know how to put on a diaper. I didn't know what kids eat or how many play groups a week a child should have."

But the moment Faith saw her daughter, named Georgica (after Faith's father, George) Swan Pond (after the pond at her house) Rose (after Faith's grandmother) Petal Qi (Skye's Chinese name) Xin (g.g.'s Chinese name) Popcorn, and nicknamed g.g. by Skye Qi, she knew she was ready to give her heart, home, and life to the child.

g.g. is now four and has flowered as the rose-petal part of her name promised. She is funny and pretty, smart and lively and speaks both Mandarin and English. Faith has bloomed as well with g.g.'s love. One of the offshoots of motherhood has been a different and deepening relationship between Faith and her sister Mechele Flaum. "She was my baby sister, seven years younger than I, so I always thought of her as my little sister," Faith said. "But now in the role of mother, a new one for me, I turned to Mechele and her husband, Sander. Mechele is a stepmother to a daughter Pamela and son-in-law Matt, who have children the age of g.g., and these are her playmates. Until now I never depended as much on Mechele, but now she is a main support. She gives me advice, and both she and Sander are there for me. When I was stuck in Chicago one night with no planes flying and a new nanny and a new puppy both due to arrive, I called Mechele.

'Don't worry,' she said easily, 'we'll be at your house. We'll stay there until you get home.' And they did."

Faith was right, of course, when she knew early on that some things would have to change. She turns down party and dinner invitations because she thinks it's more important to have dinner with g.g. She has cut back her travel schedule, but the changes are even deeper.

It isn't just that the gym in the New York town house is now a nursery; it isn't simply that instead of buying clothes for herself (Faith can scarcely remember the last time she bought something for herself) she now shops for g.g. It isn't only that her home now is a riot of pop colors (oh, where are the sleek, sophisticated colors that defined Faith's homes?). And it is beyond Faith's incessant new-mother questions about schools and neighborhoods and playmates.

The real change has come about because g.g. has caused Faith to refocus her life, deepening and enriching her relationship with her sister Mechele and Mechele's family, as well as with her best friend Lys. Wistfully, Faith says, "I wish that my grandmother Rose were here to see g.g. It was my grandmother who took care of me, because my

parents were both attorneys who worked, and she was always available. I wish she were here to see me as a
mother. And yes, I wish my parents could see this. They
would have gotten it and understood that my darling g.g.
is a continuation of our Chinese years; g.g. is carrying on
our tradition."

WHAT DO WE TELL
THE CHILDREN?

For four months Trish had awakened with a start. Even before she opened her eyes she remembered something was wrong, terribly wrong. And then slowly, sadly, her heart would go back to that terrible day when Will walked into the kitchen, threw a cardboard box on the counter, and shrugged. "There it is, Trish. Fifteen years of my life, and it all fits in one shoe box."

Trish had shaken her head in disbelief. "You mean—?" She had been unable to finish the sentence.

"It means I'm fired, canned, got a pink slip. Me, married, kids, a house, a mortgage. This morning I went to my job the same way I have for fifteen years, and as of this afternoon I'm out. About two o'clock today my boss and the company attorney came into my office and told me to pack up and leave for good by five o'clock. They read off my benefits. It wasn't just me, Trish. They did this to two hundred people today. Two hundred people went to work today thinking they had a future, and by five o'clock all we have is a past."

. . .

THE FIRST weeks Trish played the cardboard wife. She stood by her man and said things that had been in her heart for years, thoughts about how good and smart and honorable she knew her husband to be. Even though she knew her opinion wasn't going to get Will a next job, she sensed that her words brought them closer.

Then one day Trish heard their son say that he didn't see why he had to work so hard in school because he'd only lose his job someday anyway. Their five-year-old confided to Mommy that she knew Daddy must have done something wrong, so she wanted to bake some cookies for Daddy's boss so he'd forgive him and take him back.

Trish sat down with the children and explained that Daddy had really been a star. He'd gone to dinners where he was honored, and he'd gotten pay raises and letters of commendation. Even now his boss was recommending him. But she could see that wasn't cutting it with the kids.

FINALLY, one morning when Trish awoke, she realized for the first time that she wasn't sad. She was mad. Who said that she had to take this blow to her family without fighting back? She hurried the children off to school, sat down, and wrote a letter to the chairman of the corporation bitterly protesting the lack of humanity at the multibillion-dollar multinational company. The chairman never answered, but a few days later a call came from a company vice president, the head of human resources. He asked Trish to come in to see him.

Trish put aside her soccer mom outfit, dug in the closet for a trim suit, and took a train to the city. She didn't tell Will where she was going, because she wasn't sure how he'd react. She decided to see what happened and then share the news.

What happened was a sort of corporate sweet talk. "But we've done so much for Will. We gave him outplacement service, paid for an office for him to work from, helped prepare his résumé."

Trish listened and said nothing until the director of human resources said, "I think what we did was quite humane. We didn't think it was right to give him notice and then keep him for thirty or ninety days. That would have meant maintaining a kind of corporate death row. Everyone would see offices filled with about-to-be-ex-employes. That's just not good for company morale."

"What about *our* morale?" Trish cried out. "You didn't

think about the people you were firing and the families you were hurting. All you thought about was how it would look if people outside the company talked to men and women like Will. But if Will had been told what was going to happen, he could have prepared me, told the children so they'd understand. What you've done to Will will be undone as soon as he gets a new job, and I know he'll get one because he's really good. But what you've done to my family can't be changed. I'll hate you forever because of this. Don't you people understand you didn't fire one person? You fired a family that honored and respected our chief breadwinner."

The director put his hands together and formed a small bridge with his fingers. "Perhaps we'll do things differently next time," he said at last.

"So will we," Trish snapped. "Maybe next time we won't think that unpaid overtime is a company's right."

That night Trish told Will about her trip to the city. At first he was annoyed with her. "Stop being so loyal to the company that tried to destroy us," she begged. "We're the ones who are going to fight for you. Don't you see, Will? All this time you thought the company was like family.

Honey, if I've learned anything from this it's that when trouble comes, only family is family."

IT TOOK another six months for Will to find a job. The new position meant that the family had to move to a city 800 miles away. "I'm leaving with mixed feelings about everything except my family," Will admitted. "I know they're all for me, and this time I'm not going to miss dance recitals and school assemblies. If that kind of family time doesn't work for the new company, then at least I feel now that I'm able to find a job——so I'll just find another one. It's the family I can't replace."

NOT A WORD ABOUT
THIS, MOTHER

In Philadelphia they used to say that Marciarose was as well known as the Liberty Bell. Certainly more people saw Marciarose each day than saw that other landmark, because for many years Marciarose was the town's most popular newscaster on the town's most popular television station.

Married and the mother of two, she lived a life that not only straddled home and career but encompassed a lifelong passion for the arts, reading, and community involvement. It was the kind of life that sounded too good to be true and, for a while, it was.

The first glitch, a small disappointment, came when son Jonathan decided to stay in California after graduating from college. "So far from home," she said sadly to her husband, Jerry Shestack, who reminded her that since Jon wanted to write and ultimately produce films, California was the place he'd have to live.

The second bump came a few years later when Jonathan's parents realized that his relationship with a California woman was not meant to be a brief affair. For Jonathan and Portia, the woman in his life, it was love with a capital *L,* and that put the final seal on any dreams Jon's parents had that someday he'd return to what they called home. "It's what he wants, so it's what we want," his parents told each other with that kind of stiff resolve mothers and fathers assume when they put family harmony first.

As time went on, Marciarose and Jerry realized that the marriage really was what they wanted for their son. They'd never seen him so happy, so comfortable with life, so full of plans. He was about to produce his first movie when he called his parents to tell them the big news. He and Portia were also producing their first child.

Marciarose and Jerry went to see their new grandchild when he was just a few hours old. "Dov is the most beautiful child I've ever seen," Marciarose said to Jerry, "and I promise I'll say that only to you, the family, and my seven hundred closest friends."

All seven hundred—plus a few thousand more—laughed and delighted in the family's happiness. Then, just before Dov's first birthday, both Dov's parents became increasingly aware that something, something indefinable, was not quite right with the child. But what could it be? As Jon told his parents, "I saw my child vanishing before my eyes." Like her son, Marciarose was concerned, and ever the interviewer, she decided to ask a few questions of one of the medical experts she knew. And then she went to California to visit.

One afternoon as Jon and Marciarose were driving to his office, Marciarose decided to tell Jon of her suspicions and the questions she'd asked a friend. Jon became incensed. "I don't want you to talk about Dov to anybody," he snapped. "Not a word about this, Mother."

Marciarose sank silently back. Her heart ached for her son and her grandson. "All right, Jon," she half-whispered. "Remember, though, that he's my grandson, but if you don't want me to talk to anyone, I won't."

Two days later Marciarose was back in Philadelphia when she received the call from Jon. "I was wrong, M.R.," he confessed, reverting to his boyhood name for his mother. "Talk to anyone you want. We all think he may be autistic, and we are going to get another opinion now."

Holding tight to one another and their child, Portia

and Jon went to the doctor for the second opinion, and he confirmed their worst fears.

"What can we do?" Jon pleaded.

"Go home and cry and hold each other because there is nothing you can do," answered the doctor.

Portia and Jon both stiffened at an answer they felt to be unnecessarily brutal. They refused to believe that there was nothing to do.

Together they decided the one thing they could do was to start an organization to do research on autism. But desire could not replace knowledge; they knew they had a lot to learn. Portia began by going to the library for medical books and to the Internet for current information. Almost immediately, they learned that they were not alone. There were 400,000 autistic patients, but few people talked about the condition. Although autism was originally thought to be caused by cold and uncaring mothers, it was now determined that autism was not psychiatric in origin but rather neurological.

"I still don't know enough about this to do anything meaningful," Portia confessed to Jon. "I am going to take some courses."

He looked at her in amazement. "What can you learn?"

"I'm going to take courses in molecular biology, and I'm going to put my career as story editor on hold."

After a few months, Jon listened in awe to his wife. She was now conversant with the latest thinking on autism and had, in Jon's opinion, totally reinvented her brain in order to comprehend a world she'd never known.

At that point Jon joined Portia and took courses, not to gain medical information but rather to study fund raising so that together they might be a team to make a difference.

Marciarose and Jerry listened to the young parents. "We want to be a part of this," they told them.

"Raise money," John said simply.

So Marciarose, with her long list of friends, told anyone who would listen about Dov, talked about autism, explained what Portia and Jon were doing, and made friends aware that she would soon call on them to help.

The first to come forward was a longtime friend, the singer Julie Wilson. "Why don't you have a concert in your living room?" she asked. "I'll sing, you cook, and we'll see if we can raise some money for your kids."

So for the first time a fund-raising event for autism was held on the East Coast. Marciarose and Jerry proudly sent a check for $65,000 to help Portia and Jon's embryonic efforts.

In part because of this contribution, CAN (Cure Autism Now) was born, with Jon and Portia heading the organization. In addition to working full-time with CAN, Portia serves on an advisory board of the National Institutes of Health. Jon still produces feature films but also manages to run countless fund raisers and scientific conferences, lobbies Congress for more research funding, and continually enlists the help of high-profile celebrities to find a cure for this heartbreaking malady.

"In many ways this fight has become the centerpiece of our family efforts," Marciarose says. "For birthdays and anniversaries we and our friends contribute to CAN. And when our daughter Jennifer was married, some of her wedding gifts were in the form of contributions to CAN."

TODAY DOV is a part—but not the whole—of his family. Wisely, Portia and Jon determined that, despite Dov's misfortune, a family's life goes on. New life happens.

Dov now has a younger sister and a baby brother. In time they, too, will join the informed army publicly fighting to overcome autism; meanwhile they are giving their older brother the greatest gift of all: lots of hugs and everyday love.

OCCUPATION: MOTHER

Betty's father, a conservative businessman, and her mother, a stay-at-home mom, were delighted when she decided to marry Charles. "Just what I would have picked for her," Daddy said.

So the years rolled by, and in her house with the white picket fence and trellised roses, Betty was every inch the proper wife and mother. She played a role in the community, made real dinners, and became Mrs. Dutiful Mom, always available to car-pool or pick up kids of working mothers.

Then one day Betty woke up and smelled the trellised roses. And somehow she didn't like the smell.

That night, after the children had been tucked in, Betty faced Charles. "Charles, I really love you," she began, "and I love the children. But there is something else I want, too."

Charles looked up from his computer screen nervously.

"I need more from life," Betty blurted. "Charles, my life just isn't complete the way things are."

Charles looked at his wife; he was never to forget the

feeling. She looked so pretty, but she looked tense. He suspected he wasn't going to like what she said. He sensed she was going to alter their life. Oh please, he prayed inwardly, don't let her want a divorce.

Betty saw his concerned look and said quickly, "What I want is to go back to school. I want to be a lawyer."

Charles, himself a lawyer, was stunned and relieved. "Then you don't want a divorce?"

"Of course not," she answered.

That was when Charles redirected his anxiety. "But why school? You're thirty-nine," he reminded her, "and if you go back to school now, our life will never the same."

"No," she admitted soberly, "it won't. It will be even better. I'll understand what you're doing and I'll be able to talk about your cases with you."

DESPITE CHARLES'S expressed misgivings, Betty went back to school. "I hadn't felt so alive in years," she recalled. "At dinner, Charles and I got into animated discussions about the things I was learning; I was somewhat shocked to find he didn't always agree with my professors, and I'll admit that sometimes it made me angry that he thought he knew more than the teachers. The night that I gave him advice on the way to handle one of his major clients, he slept in the guest room.

"While law school was better for me, it certainly wasn't for Charles. In a sense I'd become the opposing attorney. I challenged him, and he responded by finding fault with everything, from the way I talked to the children to our grocery bills. My interests had broadened, and in many ways my life had become more focused, but I knew our marriage wasn't thriving."

Even though Betty's conservative parents now heralded their daughter's decision, Charles remained the reluctant husband. Had school been a mistake? Betty wondered.

It took another year before Betty came to realize that going to school was no mistake. The mistake had been to choose Charles's career path. "Why didn't I understand that before?" she wondered. "I'm not stupid. Why didn't I know that Charles isn't looking for competition at home? Besides, I'm not trying to make money by becoming a lawyer; what I want is to use my skills to help others."

A couple of days later Betty and Charles were getting ready to take the children to the beach. "By the way," Betty said casually as they loaded the SUV, "I've made a decision not to join a law firm."

Charles could barely hide the smile.

"Well, at least I'm not going to go to a big law firm the way you did, Charles. I've decided I'm going to work for the Legal Aid Society and help people who don't have the funds to get the legal advice they need."

Charles put his arm around her and kissed her. "That's a great idea, honey."

BETTY HAS never regretted either of her decisions, the one that sent her to school or the one that caused her to eschew the traditional legal career. "We live in a world where women like to think they can have it all," she said recently. "The thing is that if you're a mother and a wife, you can't necessarily pursue the same path as a woman with no commitments. Family harmony matters. A good marriage gives kids a real family sense. I guess we women just have to understand that once we choose to be wives and moms, that's what we'll be no matter how much education we have."

Betty has managed to have both career and marriage, and maybe there's a life lesson there. Perhaps the real answer for compatibility between a two-career couple is to redefine *having it all* so that it never means "competitive."

ARE YOU
CHERYL DOE?

Cheryl had never had a child, yet she knew. She didn't have morning sickness and her body didn't feel that different. But her heart seemed to beat with a new excitement; her heart told her that she was pregnant. Almost from the moment she sensed a new life stirring within her, Cheryl bonded with her baby. Her secret baby. She'd wanted to tell Scott, but she knew that if she did he'd make arrangements for an abortion before she could say, "No abortion, thank you."

It wasn't as if Scott were married to another woman; he wasn't, never had been, and he'd said again and again that he never wanted a child. Scott was what the gossip columns called the perennial bachelor of the season. He was president of his own company, rich and good-looking, and he knew that every time he walked into a room, even the most beautiful of the beautiful people would take a second look. Scott enjoyed being lionized as a great catch. "He's the biggest trout in the lake," Cheryl's sister, Laurie, said, "and you've hooked him."

But Laurie didn't know that her sister was pregnant; she wasn't aware that Cheryl was the one on a hook.

Although Cheryl was pretty, she wasn't rich and she wasn't society. And Cheryl knew those facts were enough to keep Scott fishing in that big lake. For about five minutes Cheryl considered telling Scott her secret (she never thought of it as *their* secret), but common sense prevailed over romance. She kept quiet, and two months later she was happy that she did, because Scott took her to dinner one night and said casually, "I've been thinking, Cheryl, that maybe we ought to cool our relationship. You know, I like my freedom, and I don't want to complicate my life with a serious—"

Cheryl interrupted, and as much as she wanted to disagree, she heard herself say, "I've been thinking exactly the same thing." And that was the minute that Cheryl made the decision she knew she would have to make. She was going to give birth to this baby, and she would keep her secret. Only Laurie would know.

WHATEVER YOU want to do, I'm on your side," Laurie told Cheryl.

"Let me think about this for another month," Cheryl

said. During that time the sisters talked. One day Cheryl planned to keep the child; the next she would shake her head and say no. At the end of the month, she said to Laurie, "I have enough money to have the baby, to stop working for a year, but I don't have enough to stop working and take care of a child, and it just isn't fair. I'm going to give the baby up for adoption. Promise me that I won't see the child after the birth; I don't even want to know if it's a boy or girl. But this was a child conceived in love, and it should have pretty good genes, so let's give life a chance."

Cheryl was a writer who dealt with editors by mail and phone, so few people saw her. Only Laurie was with her through her pregnancy, and Laurie helped her make the arrangements for the birth and adoption.

When the baby was born, Laurie kept her promise to her sister. She never told her the sex of the child, and she made sure that Cheryl never saw the daughter who was born to her.

CHERYL WENT back to her life and started seeing other men, and a year or two later Scott called. From time to time they went out together. And so the years—one, ten,

◆ · 97 · ◆

twenty—rolled by. Only Laurie knew that Cheryl had had a child. It was the sisters' secret.

And then one night, almost twenty-two years from the date of the baby's birth, Cheryl was getting ready to go out to dinner with Scott. She was just taking the hot rollers out of her hair and juggling the phone when she heard a female voice say, "Are you Cheryl Doe?"

Another call asking me to change my phone service, Cheryl thought. "I really don't have time right now," she said brusquely.

Then the voice took on a quiet, low tone. "Just answer this question, please. Does this date matter to you? September 14, 1978?"

"Yes," Cheryl said. She sank into a chair, dropping the rollers on the floor.

"Then I have a question. Are you my mother?"

Cheryl could not speak.

But the woman on the other end of the phone could not stop speaking. "I have been looking for you for four years, and I want to see you."

"Let me think about this," Cheryl answered. "I never expected this to happen."

"It almost didn't. The records were supposed to be

sealed, but I learned your name because I read it upside down when I went to——"

"Never mind," Cheryl said, fighting tears of fear and joy. "I really have to think about this. But tell me the one thing I always wanted to know. Your parents, the people who brought you up, are they—were they good to you?"

"They are very good people, and I love them. I've lived all my life right here in St. Louis, the place where I was born and just a few miles from you. My name is Heather, and I want to know my real parents. Please let me."

"I can't answer that right now. This is a call I never expected. Give me your number," Cheryl said, "and I will get back to you in a few days. I have a lot of thinking to do about this."

CHERYL CALLED Laurie. "Are you sitting down?"

"Yes."

"My daughter just called, Laurie. Did you know the baby was a girl?"

"Yes, I always knew," Laurie answered. "What are you going to do, Cheryl?"

"The first thing I'm going to do is cancel my dinner tonight with Scott. I need to think."

"We don't have any plans this evening. I'll be right over," Laurie promised.

The sisters talked for hours; finally Cheryl knew what she would do.

The next morning she called Scott and asked him to come to her apartment because she needed to talk to him about something important to both of them.

Scott was hesitant when he came to her home. Did she want marriage at this late date? Had she met someone else and was she going to ask him to exit from her life?

Cheryl poured a drink for Scott, sat down facing him, and said solemnly, "I am going to tell you something that may change your life forever or it may mean nothing at all to you."

"Yes?"

"Scott, you have a daughter. That is, we have a daughter."

He put his drink down. "What are you talking about?"

"I'm talking about a baby that I had—that we had—September 14, 1978. It was a girl, although I never knew until yesterday, when she called me. She looked up her birth certificate and accidentally learned my name. So she just looked in the phone book, found me, and called. She doesn't know you're the father so she doesn't know that—"

"Why didn't I know about this, Cheryl?"

"You probably don't remember the time, but I became pregnant just when you told me that you wanted space, or whatever it was that people wanted twenty-two years ago, and we agreed to give ourselves a kind of vacation from each other. I couldn't tell you about the baby then."

"What is she like? What does she do?"

"I don't know. All I know is that she lives here. I have her phone number, but I am asking how you want to handle this. I don't want to make you available for unwelcome publicity and I don't want to hurt her, even though I don't know her yet."

"Are you going to see her?"

"Yes. I've decided to call her and meet her, but I want to give you a choice before I see her. You don't have to tell me now. You can think about it and let me know within a week."

Scott shook his head slowly. "This is a real shock."

"It is to me, too. I didn't even know the baby's sex."

"Then how did you manage all this?"

"Laurie was with me. She knew."

"Why didn't you tell me before?"

"What was there to tell you? Now I've decided to tell you because there are decisions affecting our daughter's life you must make. The first is to ask if you want a child or not?"

Scott was quiet for a few minutes. "I never expected to have a child, but I am curious. I don't think you should have the responsibility of meeting her alone, so I'll meet her with you."

"No, Scott. That's not what I want to do. I've let you make the decisions about you and me for many years, but this is one time when I want to set the stage for meeting—" She paused. "For meeting Heather. That's her name."

"I want my daughter," he said.

"You're becoming territorial about a girl you've never met," Cheryl said. "What if you don't like her?"

"I will. She's me; she's us."

WHEN CHERYL called Heather, she arranged for the young woman to come to her apartment for tea. When she saw Heather, Cheryl gasped. She was looking at herself twenty years earlier.

She learned that her daughter was a college senior, had been a high school cheerleader (just like Cheryl), loved Chopin and country music (so did Cheryl), was very good in English, and struggled with math and science (as Cheryl had).

"I do have another question," Heather began tentatively.

Cheryl nodded. "You want to know who your father is."

"I do. That's right."

"You'll be surprised when I tell you his name, but he knows about you now. He didn't when you were born. Now that I've told him, he wants to see you as soon as you can make yourself available." Then Cheryl handed Heather Scott's business card.

Heather gasped. "He's one of the richest men in St. Louis."

"He's never been married, never had a child. But I want to tell you before you meet him that he's never supported me—never paid for your birth, because I never asked him. He's been in my life because I've made no demands. I expect you to be your own person with him, too."

WHEN SCOTT met Heather, he wept with joy. "I never dreamed I'd feel like this," he choked. "I didn't know what being a father meant. This is the most exhilarating experience of my life."

It was also a life-changing event for Scott. He immediately stopped seeing any woman other than Cheryl. Although they have not married, they have publicly acknowledged their daughter.

"Heather is what was missing in my life," Scott now admits, "but I never knew until she came to us. I don't resent Cheryl's not telling me about her, and I don't think I would have been much of a father to a little girl. But I'm certainly going to be the best father I can to a grown girl. It may be late, but it's certainly better than never. As surprised as Heather is to learn who we are, the greatest surprise to me is finding that I am a family man, after all."

DESIGN FOR LIVING

If family harmony could be designed,
Great artists would have the best families.
But since harmony is the result of
Work and thought and care,
There is a chance for all of us.

Part Three

The Legacy of Love

THE FAMILY

Lois Wyse Guber
(Grandmother)

THE WYSE FAMILY   Denise, mother
Rob, father
Stephanie, age 10
Alex, age 7
Emily, age 4

THE GUBER FAMILY   Heidi, mother
Zev, father
Marisa, age 12
Elizabeth, age 8
Sarah, age 6

THE GOLDMAN FAMILY   Kathy, mother
Henry, father
Max, age 9
Molly, age 6

BONJOUR, LOLO

The oldest are teenagers now, the youngest can read and write.

But once upon a summer, we were a family in a way none of us can ever forget.

It all came about because— I'm no longer sure exactly how it came about. Maybe it happened because I am an only child with six boy cousins who weren't interested in me (nor I in them), and I wanted the children in my family to have real interaction with their cousins.

Maybe it came about because I was able to gather my grandchildren as a group only three brief times a year— in February for Presidents' Weekend, again in August to celebrate birthdays, and at Thanksgiving—and I didn't want us to be a holiday-only family. I wanted us to be on everyday behavior, to take some of the stress and tension from brief visiting.

The summer that Marisa, the eldest, turned ten and became our first double-digit child, I realized with both joy and sadness that time was passing much too quickly.

Yes, my babies were growing up, and I was missing

something. The something, of course, was being a part of that growing up.

Yet how could I be a part of their lives? The three families lived in three different cities, and I never really had the fun of joining their families for more than two or three days at a time. More and more I began to envy friends with daughters who lived around the corner, whose sons dropped by to say hello. More and more I began to reflect on the joy it would be to become a part of one another's lives for an extended period of time.

But how?

How could we overcome the barriers of time and distance and devote ourselves to the business of being a family, a real family, an old-fashioned down-the-street, across-the-fence family?

How could I get all of them to forget their lives of lessons and camp, horseback riding and office? How could I persuade them to come to stay with me for a month, not just a day or two, at Take Five, our family house?

I knew that even if they agreed to stay, it wouldn't take long before they would find reasons to get out of the pool and head back to their cities and their involving, evolving careers.

It took me almost two years to come up with an answer. I would forget about encouraging them to spend a month at Take Five and instead rent a house in the south of France big enough for all fifteen of us. Then let my kids find a way to leave for a day or two for a meeting! I would tell them about the plan when we got together in August.

AFTER THE LAST candle was blown on the last birthday cake, after the last child went off to the barn where the kids all stayed, the grownups were having a second cup of coffee. There was a momentary lull in the conversation, and I said in an offhand manner, "Next year I think we all ought to go to France for a month."

Nobody said anything. Then they looked at me as if they expected a tag line for the joke I'd just told. When I repeated it, they still stayed silent. Finally I said, "Well?"

Heidi was the first to speak. "Great," she said loudly, and a moment later she added, " I know a perfect house in Provence. It even feels like us."

Heidi is our family Francophile. Her father, an army officer, was stationed in France the first years of her life, and she speaks French fluently. Recently, she had checked available house rentals in France for another side of the family considering a trip. That family eventually decided not to take the trip, but Heidi still had her list of houses and knew the areas and what was available.

But despite Heidi's instant enthusiasm, I could read "no" on some faces.

Heidi ignored those looks. Instead she talked about the beauty of the area she knew, told all the reasons it would work for us.

No one had the heart to say no after that. Besides, there is nothing like a dream on top of a dream to drown naysayers.

So instead of saying no no no, my kids were saying things like How big is it? Does it have a pool? Is it old?

By evening's end, everyone was buying the dream.

Empowered by their enthusiasm, I proposed taking the trip a year later, the next summer. I promised to pay for the rental of the house and the running of it (even though I still wasn't sure exactly how I'd do it). They'd be responsible for their airfares and scheduling their work lives and children's activities to accommodate our month leave. As I kept talking, I felt myself lift off and float on the wings of my dream. Somehow I knew it was all going to happen.

THE HOUSE Heidi discovered was really three separate buildings, a main house and two guest cottages, and it sounded right for what we thought we needed. So we went ahead and rented this villa in Le Rouret (don't bother looking; it's on one map in 200) from mid-June to mid-July, a time that is cheaper and less crowded than August on the Côte d'Azur. The villa is in the hills somewhere between Grasse (everyone knows the perfume city) and St. Paul de Vence (a favorite stopping place for anyone in the south of France). A stateside rental agency made the arrangements, and all through the winter we burned the fax lines as we checked airfares and worked all our airline miles in search of the cheapest of the discounted airline rates and routes.

By January I'd made the down payment on the house rental, the tickets were decided (but not paid for), and it was agreed we'd also rent three cars for the three families. Somebody would have to take Grandma as a passenger in the mother-in-law seat, because I was not planning to drive alone in France.

As the plans escalated I began to wonder. If this lovely French family was willing to rent their country house, shouldn't I also rent our house in the country? I called the dear real estate agent who'd sold the house to Lee and me and asked her to find a family to rent our house for the summer. If she didn't find a proper renter, we'd go anyway. But a franc is a franc, and why not try?

Now the momentum was propelling us all.

Oh, there were glitches here and there.

For one almost fatal moment someone thought maybe it should be done without kids. (I decided to hang tough. If there are no kids, there'll be no parents, I said.)

Henry's dad was ill. Could Henry leave? (Yes, he decided finally, after painfully wrestling the issue with all his family.)

Rob and Zev were absorbed in building their own businesses. Neither would give himself a month of vacation time. (Good, we said. Then give yourself two weeks. They agreed.)

At one point Marisa and Stephanie, the two oldest, heard about the trip as their parents discussed it (we had all agreed not to tell the children until February, but I don't think my family is too good at secrets). Both girls thought they wanted to do other things. One look from their mothers, and other plans were never again mentioned. By February, when the family got together for the annual President's Weekend vacation, we showed pictures of the house and told the grandchildren as a group of our plan. They didn't quite comprehend, but now the enthusiasm of the older girls (those same girls who'd earlier expressed doubts) convinced the younger ones, and everyone was excited.

A summer in France as a family.

A movable home.

It was getting more real every day. Days later our house in the country was rented and the financial pressure eased.

I TOLD FRIENDS what we were about to do, and more than one said, "Fifteen to France? You're crazy."

But I knew I wasn't crazy when four-year-old Emily said, "*Bonjour, Lolo,*" whenever I called.

WELCOME TO
PARADISE

Taking a long trip with children is a lot like having a baby. It's hell when it's happening, but you forget all about it once you start making memories.

We lost luggage (but we didn't lose any kids).

We missed connections (who ever said it was easy going to Kennedy Airport during rush hour?).

We made one small travel mistake (no one told us that if one family flew to Paris and then to Nice, that family would not arrive at the same terminal as the families who flew to Nice via London).

Our trip was probably no better and no worse than any trip taken by thirteen frisky optimists (remember the two fathers who came later?). There is nothing like a fifteen-hour nighttime air trip in coach to turn joking optimists into a group of slightly testy, hungry, sleep-starved kids and parents.

And our ride to the villa wasn't any scarier than any ordinary Frenchman's mad drive over narrow, twisting hilly roads. (When even the kids tell the driver to slow down, you know it's *formidable, mais vraiment.*)

But oh, the house.

It had photographed beautifully, but it took our breath away when we saw it. It was at least three beats better in life. There were indeed, as promised, three separate living spaces: the main house, a small guest house, and a pool house. There was also a beautiful pool. But most of all, there were trees and plantings that the camera had not captured. Who knew there was to be a hedge of rosemary? Who guessed that pots of flowers and herbs were everywhere? Who could have imagined a trellised patio with climbing vines? Who expected to see a still-life wherever we turned? We felt so at home that within minutes we had our first cut knee and had applied our first Band-Aid.

And that first night when I went to bed, there on the table in my room was a tiny paper vase with "Gradma" (sic) written on it, and it held three little wildflowers along with a note saying, "I love you." And so it was to sleep with the realization that eight children were tucked in all round me and would be there for a whole month. I wanted to think about that and rejoice in the sense of family. Instead I fell asleep.

Well, why not? It was my vacation, too, and when you're on vacation, there's always tomorrow. And tomorrow. And tomorrow.

TROUBLE IN PARADISE

We all agreed that this indeed was Paradise, but the first full day began with trouble in Paradise.

One of our cottages had no hot water, and the plumber did not come. In time we were to learn that French workmen are not slaves to clock or calendar. The second Monday we were there when the pool serviceman came with his chemicals just as he had the previous Monday, and I asked if he always came on Monday. "No," he answered, "I come to this house on Tuesday or Thursday." When I tried to explain today was not Tuesday, nor was it Thursday, he shrugged and said, "Oui," assuming Americans were always satisfied with a simple yes.

Our first day was fraught with first-time problems. One of our baseball players was injured. As his mother explained, "Max's head ran into a foot."

Sensing a new freedom, the cousins reached out eagerly to one another, sometimes leaving their own siblings somewhat miffed.

But as the day unfolded, there were sweet and rewarding experiences, too.

Alex took paper and pencil and went off quietly to sketch. Without speaking, Sarah joined him with her sketch pad.

Other children, aware that they couldn't play *all* the time, brought out books and found secluded rocks to call their own reading rooms. Stephanie showed her cousin Molly how to make a ponytail.

Of course it was not all sweetness and light, but a few "time-outs" restored the bumped and bruised cousins to a comfortable level of civility.

A few shared glasses of wine did the same for the parents, so that together we could explore the sights that would, in time, become the joys of our solitude. We inhaled the rosemary, sniffed the pungent leaves of the lemon tree in our garden, and soon agreed that our favorite fragrance was the gentle scent of lavender.

At day's end, even Denise, ever the watchful and concerned mother, leaned back in her chair on the patio and said thoughtfully, "I think I just may learn to relax here."

By nightfall, peace had returned to Paradise.

COUSIN CUISINE

My husband Lee was a theatrical producer who also loved cooking. For him the kitchen was a second stage; meals were not only created, they were produced. He always did a lot of our cooking, and even though I had always cooked, I'd never been as passionate about food as he. After his death, I looked at our big professional range more often than I used it. Instead of cooking for myself, I found I carried out everything from chicken salad to Chinese. And now I was going to run a house that served three meals a day to fifteen people. No wonder that before we left for France, kind friends cleared their throats and asked gently, "What will you do about food?"

I had already considered that with the rental agent and had hired both a local French cook and a young English nanny, the latter to assist both in the kitchen and with the children. So I airily dismissed such questions with a few snappy answers, the most noteworthy being, "How tough can it be to cook when eight of the fifteen are kids?"

Now I know the answer.

It isn't tough; it's impossible. Of our eight kids, two

are vegetarians. One was a part-time vegetarian (she tried and gave up during our trip). One loves eggs, one hates eggs. One loves pasta, one doesn't eat pasta. One doesn't eat nuts, one loves nuts. Give 'em hot dogs, you say? One kid doesn't eat hot dogs, and the vegetarians won't. So what did they eat? They all ate cereal. They all ate pizza. They all ate fresh fruit. And they ate the bread faster than the *boulangerie* could bake it. Each morning we stood in line at the bakery waiting for our eight loaves of bread. And that was just the morning run. In addition to bread, we had croissants from time to time and *pain au chocolate,* which was known in our household as chocolate bread. And by dinnertime we were back for another three loaves.

Our mornings were devoted to the trek to the supermarket as well as the *boulangerie.* For me, it was back to the world of squeezing tomatoes, sniffing melons, and inspecting apples, not to mention shopping for the baskets full of staples needed: dishwashing powder, washing machine powder, soft drinks, wine, cereals (two boxes a day), preserves (two large jars every other day), coffee (half a pound a day), frozen vegetables (heavy on the French-fried potatoes), ice cream, flour, bread crumbs.

And of course, the daily ration of meat and/or fish. Our army was definitely traveling on its stomach.

Most frequently Heidi, who was able to converse with shopkeepers, went to the market with me.

The very first day we were confused because, in order to get a shopping cart, we had to deposit a franc to unlock one. And it did take some conversation on Heidi's part with several fast-talking Frenchwomen before we fully understood that the franc went into the slot before the cart could be released. And when it came time to return the cart and relock it, we found that a franc popped out. Wow! Carts were free.

"*Incroyable,*" Heidi gasped, and ever the entrepreneur, she proposed that we take this amazing idea to the United States. We could hardly wait to get back to the villa and tell the other mothers. "Oh that," Kathy responded with a wave of her hand when we told her. "We have those in Philadelphia. That's probably where it came from."

Our cook, Josette, was introduced to us our first morning by our real estate agent. The agent then promptly disappeared, and we were on our own *avec* Josette. The first thing she did was to look over our carefully selected groceries and promptly proceed to tell us—in French—how badly we had shopped. She would do the shopping, she informed us. She would also prepare the menus and the shopping lists. All we had to give her was money. After all, she was French, so she knew all the little places to get all the best food. That sounded swell, but by the end of the first week I realized that while this was walking-around-shopping money to Josette, it looked more like France's war debt to me. I called the agent. Carefully, I explained (in France I was to learn that all explanation is careful) that we would have to do our own marketing and that our agent would have to tell Josette that the glory days of her shopping had ended, and she would have to make do with the kind of food we bought.

The day Josette heard the news she arrived at our house in what might best be described as a French twist. She fussed and fumed and asked to speak to Heidi, the only one of us American primitives who might have the grace to respond to her culinary needs. She explained to Heidi—in French—that we didn't know anything about food and how to buy it. But Heidi answered that we love to shop and wanted the experience of shopping as a family. After all, if you've never stood with members of your family and watched a fish being filleted you haven't truly bonded.

In the end Heidi worked her magic and Josette agreed to let us shop, provided she could continue to tell us what we did wrong.

But of course. Or as we said with a Gallic shrug as we amicably opened another bottle of red wine, "She's French."

The funny thing is that none of us really drank much wine before we went to France. Indeed, none of us drank very much in the way of spirits either, but there was something about the lazy days and sweet nights that seemed made for wine.

To be blunt, the prices seemed made for wine, too. The first time I went to the supermarket and came back with wine for less than $5 a bottle (and what good wine it was!), everyone was amazed.

Next day Rob went to the market and came back with wine that was just as good for less than $4.

Zev shopped the next day. Good wine. Great price.

By week's end we had the consumption of wine up and the price down. Of course we were aware that only a few

miles from where we sat uncorking our nonvintage wine
that was cheaper than Coca-Cola, the greatest wines in
Europe were being bottled.

But we were willing to bet that those oenophiles
weren't enjoying their château wine as much as we loved
our wine at a price.

And each night, as we polished off the last of the second or third——or was it the seventh——bottle of wine, we
leaned back, toasted Josette, and agreed the dinner was
superbe. Even if it wasn't, all four of us women smiled
with delight knowing that we hadn't cooked it.

SHOPPING ITALIAN-STYLE

Although Josette often frustrated us, Wendy, our English nanny, delighted us. She was a young girl between semesters at university, and she not only had endless patience with the kids, she spoke to them in English. She talked to the grown-ups, too. After one of our sightseeing days, a trip to Eze, Wendy looked at the bracelets we were all wearing and said, "Oh, you've been to the beach." No, we told her. We went to Eze.

"But what about the beach?" Denise asked, ever anxious to uncover a bargain——with or without sand.

"There are vendors on the beach who sell stuff."

"Anything really interesting?" Kathy asked.

"Well"——now our Wendy really warmed to the subject——"if you really want great stuff, you have to go to Ventimiglia on a Friday morning."

"Venti-who?" I asked. "And where is it?" I never drove while we were in France. You don't think I'm going to go back to a stick shift after all this time, do you? But I loved asking directions.

"It's in Italy," Wendy told us, "and I've gone there. It's lots of fun. It's just beyond Monte Carlo, and if you take the toll road, it will take you just over an hour to get there."

"This Friday?" Heidi asked, turning to Kathy and Denise and me.

"Yes," we said in unison. In our opinionated family, there wasn't a lot said in unison. When it comes to shopping, however, we women were usually on the same side.

Friday morning we spun the kids through breakfast, said goodbye to the husbands, and left them to plan the children's day along with Wendy.

The four of us climbed into the Espace as giddy as teenagers free of parents.

"Wendy says to buy leather," Kathy told us.

"I don't want leather. In fact, I don't want anything," I told them, "but I'll look."

"I'll buy some gifts," Denise said. "I still don't have anything for my mother." We all nodded. We had spent days looking at museum gift shops for gifts for Denise's family but hadn't yet found anything she thought suitable. Heidi, the driver, took her eyes off the road to announce she would definitely buy something, she just didn't know what it would be.

Ventimiglia is one of the ugliest cities in the world in one of the most beautiful countries in the world. Although it stands on the Italian Riviera, it looks no more like Portofino or Rapallo than Batman looks like Cindy Crawford.

We approached the city coming off the toll road only to find ugly barracks-style housing along a railroad track. "There's a parking lot," I said to Heidi. It was apparent to me that there wasn't going to be a lot of parking; there wasn't a lot of town, and what there was seemed to be on the other side of the railroad track.

"No," Heidi countered, "I never park at the first place. I would rather spend another ten minutes in the car to get the lay of the land. Otherwise I'll just go ahead and park, and forty minutes later after we walk and walk, we'll learn we did the wrong thing."

So we drove fifty feet, reached the railroad crossing and, of course, at that moment the gates came down.

For thirty hot minutes, we fantasized about the bargains we were missing. When the guard rails finally went up, we crossed the track and, like jockeys riding a horse to the finish line, we urged her to turn left immediately and get to the heart of the town. "I can't," Heidi moaned. "There's a sign that says no left turn." We groaned as she turned right and crossed a bridge.

"Oh my God, we left the city, and we haven't even been there," Denise cried.

"We're going in a circle," Kathy said. "You come into the city and they make you take a bridge to go around and go back to where you were. The only difference is that you're facing the other way."

And that's how we ended up in the first parking space we'd seen forty minutes earlier. Relieved to be parked, we wasted no time rushing to the flea market, and when we walked down the first fair-like aisle, we turned to one another with the same kind of dejected look. Kathy shrugged and observed, "It's Kmart." Indeed almost all one could see were the same pots and pans we see in the States, but here they cost twice as much. Gucci? Armani? Fendi? Where were the Italians we knew and loved?

"Where's the good stuff?" Denise asked. Nobody answered. We didn't know. Instead we walked and we walked.

And finally we found the good stuff.

Gloves. Wonderful gloves, and we all bought enough for the next six years. Of course, within six months I would lose my bargain Ventimiglia gloves just as fast as I lost my retail Saks Fifth Avenue ones.

Kathy bought a genuine Hermés handbag——everything was genuine except the price. Oh well, maybe the bag wasn't exactly genuine, but who's to know? It's leather, and it's gorgeous.

Heidi bought a tablecloth, and we all bought scarves and belts for very few American dollars or French francs. We did best with the vendors who took Visa cards.

On the way out we found the Cartier salesman. Just because his wares were on the ground and he talked faster than a TV pitchman, would you think it wasn't really Cartier? Kathy and Heidi bought belts for their husbands (one thought it was okay; one said he'd never wear it).

But as I looked at the fantastic Cartier goods, I saw it— that perfect new little Cartier watch I'd seen in New York. I don't need a watch any more than I need more grand-children. Still, who can't love one more?

How much, I asked?

By the time we got it down to $20, I decided it was worth the effort. Besides, it had a leather band, and that's worth $20 right there, I told the girls. "Well, if *you* think that's leather . . ." one said.

We stopped for sandwiches and beer, had gelato, and agreed we'd have to come back to Ventimiglia someday.

Meanwhile, we could go back to the villa and brag to the husbands that we'd been to Italy.

And by the time we got back to the house I had the perfect proof of our trip: one gorgeous nonfunctioning Cartier watch.

FRENCH LIGHTS

There was a soft rhythm to life in Le Rouret; for me it often began with a walk up and down our hilly roads, then breakfast on the terrace followed by the day's planned adventure. Our highlight was dinner for the grown-ups, made and served by Josette, and fiercely praised by all four women. By eleven o'clock——thanks to the cool air, the dinner, and the wine——we were all ready for a sweet sleep.

Sleep came quickly and was rarely interrupted for any of us. Yet one night I woke suddenly at 3:00 A.M. to lights blazing in my room. Befuddled and bemused, I was somewhere between dream and reality. I rubbed my eyes and looked around. How could the lights go on in my room if I hadn't turned them on? What was happening in our house? Was a child in trouble? Was someone calling from the States? I got out of bed and looked around. Still the light blazed. I opened the door of my room and walked barefoot into the hall. No one was awake. No one was stirring. Even stranger, the rest of the house was dark. What electrical phenomenon had caused only the lights in my room to burn? A signal from on high or a faulty wire from below? I went back into my room to consider the possibilities for action. Although it was a warm night, I began to shiver with that vague concern that comes when, in unfamiliar surroundings, the unexpected occurs. Should I call one of the adult children? Where were the fuse boxes? Why was this friendly house betraying me?

I went to the light switch to turn the lights off; instead they went on. Then I began to laugh. Those weren't the electric lights burning in my room. They were the brighter-than-electric lights of countless fireflies. Fireflies! I hadn't seen a firefly since I was a child. Had childhood, like Peter Pan himself, flown in my open windows?

The next morning, I told the children about my flying visitors, and that night we found a thicket filled with fireflies outside the guest house where Max and Molly were staying, and all of us waited for dark so that we might stand together to watch their magical night lights. I, who have seen the lights of Paris and London and New York, stood captivated and watched in silence as the enraptured faces of my grandchildren glowed in the firefly light.

Fireflies, however, were not our only flying visitors. In the beginning, when I saw the first mosquito in my bedroom, I assumed that this mosquito would make infrequent appearances, a little like a relative who knows he can be tolerated for short periods but is not welcome for an extended stay. But our mosquito not only stayed, he brought relatives.

The children were the real victims. They would awake in the morning scratching and complaining of itchy bites everywhere. We told them to sleep in long-sleeved T-shirts, stay under the covers, and wear slippers. That didn't fool the mosquitoes, and within days the innocuous-looking bites had been scratched into major battle wounds.

Off to the *pharmacie* went a parental platoon to buy not only another six packages of Band-Aids but to search for something to alleviate the itches. They bought the pharmacist's first, second, and third choices. The itching continued. So we changed *pharmacies*. Seven *pharmacies* later, the sound of scratching could still be heard on our land.

One parent suggested we try something to let the mosquitoes know they were not welcome. And so we bought a series of household sprays and finally a kind of electrical bomb that plugged into a wall socket and emitted an odor that was guaranteed to repel mosquitoes without asphyxiating humans.

But the mosquitoes proved to be bombproof. And Baby Emily, obviously the most edible of all us humans, looked as if she had a rash, so bitten was she. Days later her father, who was in training for the New York marathon, arrived with a small suitcase filled with his running clothes and all kinds of unguents, including Ben-Gay. He decided, since all else failed, to rub it all over Emily.

After that the mosquitoes left. Maybe the real problem was that our mosquitoes had aching muscles.

THE GENTLEMAN
CALLER

When my friend Florence heard about our family trip, she showed immediate enthusiasm, because she and her husband, Bob, were planning to visit the south of France in July with their thirteen-year-old grandson and thought it would be an added adventure to visit us.

"Perfect," I responded. "We have an almost-thirteen-year-old girl. Maybe they can play together." You'd think I'd never read *Lolita* or heard that s-e-x is an international word meaning boys and girls.

So when Florence called one day—a local call—I knew we were about to have visitors. "Come for lunch to-morrow," I said easily. "Nothing fancy. Just family. Bring bathing suits. The kids will hang out at the pool, and we'll sit around." And then I got busy with our day.

That night, as we all sat on the terrace and waited for the night sounds and the fireflies, I remembered we were to have guests. "My friends Florence and Bob are going to stop here tomorrow for lunch."

"Do they live here?" Stephanie wondered.

"Visitors. Like us," I answered. "Oh, and by the way, they have their thirteen-year-old grandson with them."

Marisa, our almost-thirteen-year-old, screamed.

Was it joy? Was it fear? How would I know? I'm not twelve going on forty-two.

That night there was a lot of back-and-forthing between the girls' house and the main house. "What's going on?" I asked Stephanie as I glimpsed her racing up the stairs in the main house.

"Makeovers," she responded breathlessly.

Heidi came downstairs. "It's about the boy," she hissed.

"What boy?" I wondered.

"Your *boy*," she explained. "Your friend Florence is bringing a *boy*."

I couldn't believe it. These cute little girls were going bananas because a b-o-y was coming to visit. I opened my mouth to speak. I was about to say, "But we are in France, and this is not what the trip is about. Why should you adorable girls want to be anything but yourselves? Why do you want to change perfection?"

Fortunately, I kept quiet.

Throughout the trip, I was to learn that I would never regret a single moment when I kept quiet.

The grandson arrived with his grandparents and we met them at the post office in Le Rouret because no one without a guide dog and a thousand years of French ancestry could ever find our house without help.

Our car, the workaday Espace, led the way, and Bob, Florence, and Handsome Grandson followed in a Mercedes.

My newest advice for an adult who wants to make a hit with teenagers is to present them with teenagers of the opposite sex who arrive via Mercedes.

The kids did not need any of us when they met. They went off to the pool, although Florence did fuss for a few minutes. "Do you have a towel?" she asked her grandson. From the look he gave his grandmother, she might as well have asked if he brought his water wings.

The girls fluttered a bit and then settled down to being themselves. I knew they were all fine the minute I heard the first scream. Grandson had thrown one of the girls—fully clothed—into the pool.

All the granddaughters then got together and gave a push. Now Grandson was in the pool——fully clothed.

This encouraged the two younger boys. They got into the pool. This was their kind of play, too.

And so the day went.

A little screaming.

A lot of laughing.

Some lunch.

By day's end, when Florence and Bob were ready to leave for St. Paul de Vence and their dinner engagement, they collected still-wet Handsome Grandson and suggested he change into the other clothes he had brought with him. His shoes, however, were still wet. "I don't care," he said gallantly.

BY THE TIME the Mercedes wiggled its way out of our narrow drive, the girls had forgotten about their makeovers and were ready for reviews.

"What did you think of him?" I asked Marisa.

"Awfully young" was her two-word opinion.

"He seems young for his age," Stephanie, age ten, echoed.

Molly, age eight, later confided, "Boys mature later than girls, and so girls are about two years older than boys."

"How do you know?" I inquired.

"Stephanie told me," she replied solemnly.

Of course. Stephanie, who gets the scoop on life from Marisa and then passes it on, is Molly's undisputed authority.

If nothing else, France had certainly established the chain of information and communication in this family.

ISN'T FRANCE A TOPLESS COUNTRY?

Alex, age eight, came to France in search of topless beaches. Evidently the guys on the playground back in Ohio told him this was the only reason real guys went to France, so every time we went near *la plage,* Alex's eyes would light up and he would ask breathlessly, "Where are they?"

"They" were not in great evidence at the beaches we visited, and the occasional female who appeared topless did not seem to give him the kind of satisfaction he had been led to believe was waiting.

When Alex's father arrived, he reported that he had been seated on the plane next to a man who had a map of all the nude beaches in the south of France, but he had failed to take notes. Alex kept pestering me, "Can't we go to a nude beach?"

I have a standard reply. The children know that I always say yes to all their requests unless it is something I consider dangerous. So I said no. Why are nude beaches dangerous? Alex wondered. I couldn't answer at that moment.

Within days the *International Herald Tribune* published a story about a man who was burned to death while sunning on a nude beach in the south of France. I showed the story to Alex.

But the grown-ups in our house shook their heads at the suggestion of danger. They knew that man must have died with a smile.

THE FAMILY AT PLAY

Sometimes happiness is so overwhelming, we almost forget how and why we came to the moment.

One of our last nights at the house, the children presented a play for the grown-ups, a play they had rehearsed for days. I had found a book with the children's play in a bookstore just before we left and brought it along in case Molly and Alex, the two who love theater the most, wanted to do a reading together. It turned out everybody wanted to be in a play. And so the children decided to produce their own play for the parents.

It was not without its own nonscripted theatrics, however. During the week or so of rehearsal time there were tears and recriminations and screams of "Dummy," and "I didn't," and "Yes, you did." The parents wisely realized that play-acting is just another step toward playing at life. So generally they tried to keep their cool and keep their distance. When the levels of frustration and anger became too painful even for parents to hear, they intercepted, but most of the time they let the children work out their annoyances themselves.

Against this background we were all a little tense the days before the opening.

The day of the performance we began to relax when all the grown-ups received a written invitation. The kids might be getting it together, after all. And each of us loved the idea of being invited; privately we admitted that we were not so sure we would love the performances. After dinner, during which we fortified ourselves with an extra glass of red wine, we went down to the house where Max and Molly lived with their parents. Chairs were set up in the living area, and we were ushered to our seats. When Baby Emily came out to announce the performance, we all cheered. And then we settled back, our expectation exceeded only by our hopes. But as the play unfolded, we sat straighter in our chairs. Yes, our kids knew all their lines. And with ingenuity and originality, they had made costumes out of the nothings in each closet. But most important, they were acting together. There were no stars. They were a team. They played off each other's lines, had fetching pieces of business.

We looked at one another. Were these our kids? Where were we when they learned to work together? How had they come together to overcome their differences? How did they know they could make a success of a joint effort? We beamed at their ability to overcome whatever prickliness had existed. These children who really knew nothing had discovered everything of life together. Each child glowed with the pride of a job well done. They knew they had earned the right to their self-confidence; a secure sense of self was now a part of each. We all knew that was a gift that not even the most loving parent could ever give.

THERE WERE other memories made those weeks, some funny, some poignant.

Children were always losing something. Francs, shells, combs, toys. Books. Somebody's socks often ended up in someone else's shoes, but the most frustrating loss was Stephanie's continuing loss of her retainer. One night she left it on the table after eating, and ever-helpful Josette tossed it in the garbage, where Stephanie had to fish for it. It was not until Stephanie lost the retainer in the pool and had to dive for it herself that she managed to keep it in her mouth where it belonged.

We had a birthday picnic for our four summer birthday girls at the park in Nice, and as we drove into Nice we saw laundry flapping at every house. Made us feel right at home, because our house had no dryer ("It's not French to have a dryer," we were told). Still, outdoor drying was not unpleasant; the fresh laundry had a wondrous fragrance of its own.

And there were other smells that once sniffed would forever evoke the family summer in France: the aroma of the white flowers that greeted us every time we walked into the house through our front door; the sweet garden smells along the morning walk up and down the mountainside, particularly the fragrance of the lavender; the delicious odors from the *boulangerie* and the joy of going to the stands to buy parsley and tomatoes and garlic. Only French food tastes like French food, because the ingredients have a distinctive French accent. Only the garlic in France can play a seductive dance in the mouth; only French red wine can be bought for pennies and taste like *premier cru;* only French salads are born crisp.

Of all our sights, on the beaches we walked and the mountains we hiked, perhaps the most unforgettable scene was the day we left the children at home with our nanny, motored to Eze, walked up the steep hills over the Mediterranean, and then, like the pilgrims we felt ourselves to be, stood together in respectful silence at the sweeping view of sea and sky and hills that would sustain us in days and years to come. We hugged one another in silence and came down the mountain, and it is that distant memory that seems to grow closer with time.

WE WERE only a day or two into our stay in Provence and I was sitting on the stone terrace with a few of the granddaughters, when suddenly one of them, I can't remember which, asked me, "Grandma, did you really love Grandpa?"

"I adored him," I answered without skipping a beat. And then——and then my eyes filled with tears. I wanted to say more to the girls. I wanted to tell them that their grandfather had loved each of them. I wanted to remind Sarah that he held her in his arms just days after she was born, days before he died. But I couldn't say any of those things. I tried to speak, but nothing happened.

Then the older girls rushed to my side and threw their arms around me. "Oh Grandma," said one, "we didn't mean to make you sad."

"I'm not sad," I told them. "I'm sorry. All this should be ours, and it's only mine."

. . .

AND THAT'S the other side of the coin.

In the days to come, I thought of Lee so often.

We had come to Provence ten years earlier and had one of the best weeks of our life together. We had explored the villages and the galleries and the museums.

In the house where I live is the print he bought on that trip, a Léger from the museum in Biot, one of the places I visited again on this trip. So sweet, so sad. So difficult but so necessary.

We had lunch one day at Chèvre d'Or because Lee and I had been there and I knew he would want me to take our children.

I followed some of those remembered steps not because I was trying to resurrect my ghosts but rather because I wanted to put them at rest. Somehow I needed to see places alone that once we had traveled together.

But even though I walked alone, as the weeks went by Lee appeared often.

I heard him critiquing the cook and dismissing the kitchen itself for its lack of—can you believe it?—French knives.

I saw him on the terrace in his blue sweater, the one that matched his eyes, and he was reading and listening to music.

Sometimes he said, "Let's get out of here," and we'd leave those couples who are our children and go off for a walk by ourselves.

Most of the time, however, he kept to himself just the way he did in life. But when he thought I was overstating my position, arguing too strongly about anything, from the price of groceries to the plans for the day, he'd laugh and say, "Okay, Gonzo." And I'd stop talking.

In France I learned that memories made me miss Lee desperately. In France, with our family, I felt more alone than ever.

I was surrounded by people who have people. The children are bound to one another and beholden to their parents. Each couple is loving and interdependent, so well married that they are able to finish one another's sentences or speak their minds by exchanging a look. When I am at home in the stillness with which I live, I do not miss this kind of connection that they have. And at home my memories sustain me; they do not haunt me.

SO WILL YOU do it again? friends ask.

Probably not.

Not because I did not love the experience; I wouldn't trade it for twice the dollars or francs invested in the summer. And not because I could not sustain my enthusiasm for adventure or love for my family; both are boundless.

No, the reason I can't do another month is that as independent and self-reliant and strengthened by life as I am, I don't want to be that lonely ever again.

So I will go back to my life, alone.

And one by one my children and grandchildren will come to visit when they can or want to take time from their expanding lives of lessons, sports, camp, and other vacation opportunities. Always we will share the pictures, laugh over the memories, and remember it as a great summer.

And maybe one of the reasons that it will resonate forever for all of us is that instinctively we all know it's the kind of experience, like a real love, that happens just once in a lifetime.

ACKNOWLEDGMENTS

All families are alike in that each has at least one story that is told and retold and becomes part of family lore. Some of those stories have been passed on to me with the request that I not use actual names, and I am grateful to all of you and touched by your confidence. Some of the tellers of these tales, beginning with my mother, children, and grandchildren, as well as Joanna Simon, John Mack Carter, Marilyn Gould, Faith Popcorn, and Marciarose Shestack, spent many hours making sure I had the stories right, and I thank you for your time and effort. Others close to me who were supportive and encouraging during the five years that I was writing this book are Annelle Warwick Savitt, Phyllis Levy, Israela Margalit, Liza Antelo, Mason and Margot Adams, Hope Gropper, Michael Zimmerman, Marianne Gogolick, Sheliah Rae Gross, Terry Hurst, Kasper, Eva Pusta, Pat Rosenwald, Cindy Greenfield, Joan Benny, Nancy Whitaker, and my nephew/friend Kenneth Wyse. My loving thanks to each of you for your warmth, encouragement, and understanding.

Special thanks to Constance Herndon, the caring and capable editor who shepherded this book from inception to publication, and to her assistant Stephen Motika. My thanks once again to Owen Laster, agent extraordinaire.

How lucky I am that each of you is part of my family of friends.

ABOUT THE AUTHOR

Lois Wyse has published more than sixty books, including *Women Make the Best Friends* and *Friend to Friend*. Her *New York Times* bestselling *Funny, You Don't Look Like a Grandmother* has been made into a musical, which has its West Coast premiere at the Santa Monica Playhouse and will be seen at theaters across the country. She has been a longtime contributing editor at *Good Housekeeping* and wrote a syndicated weekly advice column called "Wyse Words" for more than a decade. The president and cofounder of Wyse Advertising, she lives in New York City and East Hampton, New York.

✦　·　✦

Printed in the United States
By Bookmasters